THE
TATA
SAGA

Foreword by
HARISH BHAT

THE
TATA
SAGA

INSPIRING STORIES FROM
A TIMELESS INSTITUTION

PORTFOLIO
PENGUIN

An imprint of Penguin Random House

PORTFOLIO

USA | Canada | UK | Ireland | Australia
New Zealand | India | South Africa | China

Portfolio is part of the Penguin Random House group of companies
whose addresses can be found at global.penguinrandomhouse.com

Published by Penguin Random House India Pvt. Ltd
7th Floor, Infinity Tower C, DLF Cyber City,
Gurgaon 122 002, Haryana, India

First published in Portfolio by Penguin Random House India 2018

Anthology copyright © Penguin Random House India 2018
Foreword copyright © Harish Bhat 2018
The copyright for the pieces vests with the individual contributors or their estates.

Page 253 is an extension of the copyright page.

10 9 8 7 6 5

The views and opinions expressed in this book are the authors' own and the
facts are as reported by them which have been verified to the extent possible,
and the publishers are not in any way liable for the same.

ISBN 9780670091751

Typeset in Adobe Caslon Pro by Manipal Digital Systems, Manipal
Printed at Thomson Press India Ltd, New Delhi

www.penguin.co.in

To 150 years of the Tata Group

Contents

Contents

Part III: Companies and Institutions

Foreword

Glimpses of the Tata Saga

'Can you name companies which are 150 years of age, or older?'

I have asked this simple question several times, in front of many diverse audiences—sometimes well-informed corporate executives, at other times bright young college students. Each time, only a few hands go up. And I hear very few answers. Then, often, there is complete silence. This is to be expected, because very few companies live beyond 150 years of age. In fact, the average life of a large global company is far shorter, between forty and fifty years.

This is one reason why the Tata saga is fascinating and inspiring. The Tata Group was founded in 1868 by Jamsetji Tata, who is revered as the Father of Indian Industry. In 2018, 150 years later, this remarkable institution is as restless and vibrant as ever.

It is the largest Indian corporate house and one of the most visible India-headquartered conglomerates in the world. It has nearly 4 lakh shareholders, employs over 700,000 people, and has a presence in over 150 countries worldwide. Over 600 million consumers around the world use Tata products and services, because of their consistent quality, enduring appeal and the trust that Tata is privileged to have earned over the years.

However, what makes Tata unique is not just its spread or size, but the reason why it exists. Over a century ago, the founder, Jamsetji Tata, set out his vision of creating an organization where the 'community is not just another stakeholder in the business, but is, in fact, the very purpose of its existence.' This vision of its founder has remained the guiding North Star for Tata.

The Tata Trusts are the best illustration of this philosophy. For the past 125 years, they have contributed to many aspects of the community around us, investing significantly in education, health, creating livelihoods, art and culture. These public charitable trusts own 66 per cent of the equity shares of Tata Sons, the parent company of the Tata Group. As a result of this unique ownership structure, a significant proportion of the profits of Tata Sons flow to the Tata Trusts, which in turn invest these funds back into the community. In the words of J.R.D. Tata, who was the chairman of the Tata Group for over fifty years, this ensures that 'what came from the people has gone back to the people many times over'.

What has made the Tata Group endure, flourish and lead for 150 years is a unique marriage between this community-centric philosophy and the pioneering spirit that has been its lifeblood. The former provides a steadfast sense of purpose and strong harmony with the community, while the latter ensures that Tata always stays relevant, and very often ahead of its time. If giving back to the community and the nation has been the guiding North Star, pioneering new enterprises has been the restless ship on which Tata has sailed towards this horizon.

Since the beginning, the Tatas have pioneered multiple businesses which are important to the nation and community. These include: India's first integrated steel plant; India's first luxury hotel; India's first commercial airline; the first Indian car; branded iodized salt, which has changed the way India consumes its food; branded jewellery, which has transformed one of the country's largest markets; the company which has put India on the global IT services map. This list is virtually endless. These pioneering businesses, each of them relevant to their day and age, have constantly fuelled the Tata ship and kept it in robust shape for 150 long years. Powered by this engine, the ship continues to sail forward confidently into the next 150 years. Its direction is clear, because its North Star has remained constant.

Steering this ship with confidence requires the firm hands of a captain. The Tata Group is fortunate to have been led by visionary captains over the years. Their stories make for some of the most gripping and inspiring chapters of *The Tata Saga*.

Men of Steel, Heart of Gold

One legendary story that has constantly inspired me is the tale of how the founder and first chairman, Jamsetji Tata, sought to establish India's first integrated steel plant in Jamshedpur. Historian R.M. Lala has beautifully narrated the story in his excellent book *The Creation of Wealth*.

Way back in the 1880s, Jamsetji Tata developed a belief that steel would be essential for the nation's development. He studied the industry thoroughly, visited locations in India which had iron ore deposits, and eventually went to Pittsburgh, the heart of the steel industry in the US, to meet the world's best metallurgical experts. There, he was warned that exploring steel manufacturing in India would cost a fortune and there was no guarantee that the endeavour would succeed. He faced scepticism from many quarters. When the then British chief commissioner of the Indian Railways, Sir Frederick Upcott, heard about this venture a few years later, he famously said: 'Do you mean to say that the Tatas propose to make steel rails to British specifications? Why, I will undertake to eat every pound of steel rail they succeed in making.'

Jamsetji Tata, like all great pioneers, was a determined man, with immense faith in the enterprise he had embarked upon. So he forged ahead, choosing to ignore the doomsayers and the cynics. With the help of an American expert, he undertook a scientific survey of the project in densely forested areas where raw material was likely to be available. The first round of exploration was abandoned because the iron ore and coal required was not available in that area. Jamsetji persisted. Eventually, his team located the required iron ore reserves in the jungles near the village of Sakchi in Eastern India, and, with the best available technology and expertise of the times, the steel plant was created there.

The plant did not produce steel during Jamsetji Tata's lifetime. Production commenced in 1912, eight years after his demise. By then, his son Dorabji Tata had succeeded Jamsetji Tata as the chairman. Steel rails from this plant were also used in the British war effort in Mesopotamia, during World War I. Around that time, Dorabji Tata is reported to have said that if Sir Frederick Upcott had lived up to his word, he would have had 'some slight indigestion'.

This inspiring story does not end here. Jamsetji Tata's vision was not merely to make steel in India, but to also create a modern township around the steel plant that served the needs of employees and residents in an exemplary manner. It is fascinating to note how he articulated this dream, in a letter that he wrote to his son in 1902—'Be sure to lay wide streets planted with shady trees, every other of a quick growing variety. Be sure that there is plenty of space for lawns and gardens. Reserve large areas for football, hockey and parks. Earmark areas for Hindu temples, Mohammedan mosques and Christian churches.' Thus, Sakchi, a small village in the wilderness, became the first planned smart, industrial city of India. Later, in 1919, the British rulers of the country named this town Jamshedpur, as a tribute to its founder.

There is an interesting postscript to this story of the creation of Tata Steel and Jamshedpur, which puts a spotlight on the role played by the second chairman of the Tata Group, Dorabji Tata. After an initial period of great success, the steel plant ran into significant difficulties and misfortunes in the post-World War I period. In 1924, driven by large debt and a fall in demand, the company was on the verge of bankruptcy and closure. At one point, there was no money to pay wages to the workers in Jamshedpur. To rescue the company, funds were urgently needed, and Dorabji Tata pledged his entire personal fortune of Rs 10 million to obtain a loan from the Imperial Bank of India. The fortune that he pledged included his wife Meherbai Tata's jewellery—including the flawless Jubilee Diamond, which, at 245 carats, was twice as big as the fabled Kohinoor. This is a tale of nerves of steel, a fabulous diamond and a heart of gold.

The epic saga of Tata Steel has continued for many decades thereafter, with many interesting new tales of bold and pioneering moves which deserve an entire book to themselves. Consider these stories of recent years: In 2012, Tata Steel was the first integrated steel company outside Japan to win the coveted Deming Grand Prize, the highest honour in quality awarded to companies for excellence in total quality management. In 2008, Tata Steel acquired Corus, a major European steel company and in a subsequent joint venture with Thyssenkrupp, announced in 2017, created Europe's second largest steel company. The massive new steel plant at Kalinganagar in Orissa, which commenced production in 2015, is one of India's largest greenfield ventures in modern times. And, most recently in 2018, the successful acquisition of Bhushan Steel is an initiative that marks the very first successful case of resolution of a large bank loan defaulter, under the country's new Insolvency and Bankruptcy Code (IBC). The 'Make in India' steel plant that Jamsetji Tata conceptualized over 130 years ago continues to flourish today. Indeed, it stands tall as one of the finest corporate institutions of our times.

Wings to Fly, Wheels to Soar

Let me narrate two other stories of the Tata chairmen, both inspiring tales of magnificent ambition. Just like the saga of Jamsetji Tata's steel plant, these stories exemplify the marriage between pioneering new businesses and a strong commitment to the nation, which has been at the heart of the Tata Group. One of these stories features J.R.D. Tata, who served as the chairman of the group for over fifty years, from 1938 until 1992. The other story features Ratan Tata, who succeeded JRD, and led the group for over two decades, since 1992.

J.R.D. Tata had a great passion for aviation. In fact, he was the first Indian to qualify as a commercial pilot. Driven by this passion, and by his belief that air transport would be critical for the nation's future, he founded India's first commercial airline, Tata Airlines, way back in 1932. He piloted the inaugural flight himself, on 15 October 1932, carrying 25 kilograms of mail in a de Havilland Puss Moth aircraft from Karachi to Mumbai. This flight is now a legend in the annals of Indian aviation.

Speaking in Mumbai after launching the airline, JRD said, 'I want to express, perhaps unnecessarily, the unbounded confidence we have in the ultimate future of air transport in India.' The then director general of Civil Aviation wrote about this venture in the national newspaper, *The Times of India*, 'Scarcely anywhere else in the world was there an air service operating without support from the Government. It could only be done by throwing on the operator the financial risk. Tata Sons were prepared to take that risk.'

Over the next few decades, J.R.D. Tata built an enterprise that placed the country firmly on the aviation map. In 1936, larger aircraft were inducted into the fleet. In 1946, Tata Airlines went public and transformed itself into Air India Ltd, the company that brought passenger air travel to India. In 1948, Air India went international, proudly taking the Indian carrier into European skies. Air India offered customers the finest flying experience, worthy of royalty, as symbolized by its loveable mascot, the Maharajah. Later, in 1953, soon after the government nationalized all private airlines, J.R.D. Tata was invited to head the international airline now owned by the state—a role he undertook with great panache and energy for the next twenty-five years.

If J.R.D. Tata pioneered commercial aviation for the nation in the 1930s, his successor, Ratan Tata, led an equally ambitious and risky venture over sixty years later, in producing India's first car. In the early 1990s, India did not have a car it could call its own, which had been both designed and produced within the country. When Ratan Tata first suggested, in 1993, the possibility of component and car manufacturers in India getting together to produce a car worthy of national pride, the idea attracted considerable scepticism.

In his own words, 'Needless to say, there was considerable criticism and cynicism about my suggestion. In the absence of a positive reaction, I decided that if we're not going to do this as a collaborative national effort, Tata Motors would undertake the lead effort. In 1995, we formally undertook a programme to develop a new Indian car. Two types of reactions were forthcoming at that stage: one was that we were being very brave but the other, which came more often, was that we were being very foolish.'

This reaction is no different from the scepticism that Jamsetji Tata faced a hundred years earlier, when he set about establishing India's first integrated steel plant. For pioneers who endeavour to break new ground, such cynicism is perhaps par for the course. Ratan Tata forged ahead with an effort that he considered important for the nation, with faith in his company's engineers, and belief in his dream.

The Tata Indica, India's very first domestically developed and manufactured car, was born in 1999. Sporting breakthrough styling for its time, the car was manufactured to exacting specifications at a new plant set up at the Tata Motors campus in Pune. This is a fascinating story, which I have had the privilege to narrate in my book *Tata Log*, and which I think every proud

Indian will enjoy reading. After some initial challenges, the Tata Indica went on to become the nation's fastest selling car in the year 2001. Most importantly, it became a symbol of Indian prowess in developing world-class products. Ratan Tata had, once again, chosen to take the group where no Indian company had gone before.

India's first integrated steel plant, circa 1880s. India's first commercial airline, circa 1932. India's first car, circa 2001. These are three different eras, separated by 130 long years and three different chairmen, spanning three generations. In each case, the motivation is to do what is important for the nation. In each case, the desire is to lead, in a bold and meaningful way. In each case, there is strong belief, personal passion and exemplary courage. So, are these actually three different stories, or merely three chapters in a single, well-woven, epic tale of the Tata saga? Into what fascinating worlds and narratives will the next chapters of this saga lead us, over the next century?

Professionals Par Excellence

The Tata Group is fortunate to have had visionary captains, in its chairmen. And it is equally fortunate to have been home to several exemplary professionals, who have been leaders of industry in their own right. Over the decades, the group has identified and nurtured extraordinary people, who have created and managed enterprises with distinction. They have, in turn, supported their chairmen in moulding the character and developing the future of this great organization.

What is striking is that these Tata professionals have been a diverse lot—technocrats, legal luminaries, economists, aviators, hard-nosed businessmen, wizards of finance and benefactors of the arts. Some have been mavericks, and others have been colourful personalities who have left behind unique imprints on corporate India. Perhaps it is because of this very diversity that these professionals have collectively provided the Tata Group the intellectual firepower required to establish leadership in so many different sectors of the economy.

Let me quickly scan the pages of history, to put before you the brief profiles of ten extraordinary professionals who have contributed to the story of the Tata Group. This is not a comprehensive list, by any means, but ten is a good, round number, to illustrate the range of outstanding professional talent that has helped mould this great institution over the decades.

Charles Perin: The history of great professionals who have served the Tata Group goes back to 1902, and to Charles Page Perin, whose services were engaged by Jamsetji Tata at the turn of the twentieth century, to conduct a scientific survey for the steel venture in India. Perin was an eminent consulting engineer of New York, strongly recommended by Julian Kennedy, who was one of the foremost metallurgical engineers in the world at that time. Like the many professionals who followed him, Perin agreed to render his services to the Tatas, travelling all the way from the US to India, because he was inspired by the vision that was in front of him.

In R.M. Lala's book *The Creation of Wealth*, there is a brief but striking narration of how Perin described his first encounter with Jamsetji Tata:

'I was poring over some accounts in the office, when the door opened, and a stranger in a strange garb entered. He walked in, leaned over my desk, and looked at me fully a minute in silence. Finally, he said in a deep voice, "Are you Charles Page Perin?" I said, "Yes". He stared at me again, silently, for a long time. Then, slowly he said, "I believe I have found that man I have been looking for. Julian Kennedy has written to you that I am going to build a steel plant in India. I want you to come to India with me, to find suitable iron ore and coking coal, and the necessary fluxes. I want you to take charge as my consulting engineer. Mr Kennedy will build the steel plant wherever you advise, and I will foot the bill. Will you come to India with me?" I was dumbfounded, naturally. But you don't know what character and force radiated from Tata's face. And kindliness, too. "Well," I said, "yes, I will go." And I did.'

This episode highlights two facets of the Tata saga. Starting with Jamsetji Tata, and until today, the Tatas have believed in engaging the best professionals. And these professionals have, in turn, been inspired to work for a group that is much more than a mere corporate. Like Perin, their inspiration to work for the Tatas has come from the 'character and force' that they see in the group and its leaders.

George Wittet: In the 1920s, when Dorab Tata decided to construct a new office building for the Tata Group, it was the famous Scottish architect George Wittet who was engaged for this purpose. Bombay House, which opened in 1924, and is still the headquarters of the Tata Group, stands proud testimony to his expertise. Wittet also famously designed some of Mumbai's best-known landmarks, including the Gateway of India and the Prince of Wales Museum. As architect for the Tatas, he led the design and planning of not just Bombay House, but forty-four significant projects—a number that exemplifies the scale and breadth of vision that has kept great professionals intensely engaged with the group.

Nevill Vintcent: In the 1930s, when J.R.D. Tata was considering a serious foray into commercial aviation, he turned to Nevill Vintcent, an expert and somewhat colourful aviator. Vintcent had previously served with the Royal Air Force, and came to India toughened by his experiences of flying and combat in hostile territories. He helped pioneer the air mail service that launched Tata Airlines in 1932. Immediately after J.R.D. Tata famously piloted the first flight from Karachi to Bombay on 8 October 1932, Nevill piloted the next leg of this flight, onward from Bombay to Madras. He then went on to partner the Tatas in building the airline company, and also transformed the nascent aviation industry in India in many other ways. Unfortunately, during World War II, an RAF aeroplane he was flying on, from England to India, disappeared without a trace, presumably attacked and shot down by enemy aircraft. But the aviation industry he helped establish has lived on, has multiplied several-fold, and propelled the country forward.

Dr John Mathai: A member of the Tata Group's leadership team in the 1940s and 1950s, Dr John Mathai was a professor and economist who drafted the famous Bombay Plan—the first-ever long-term plan for the economic development of India, published by J.R.D. Tata along with other leading Indian industrialists such as G.D. Birla and Kasturbhai Lalbhai. Between his stints with the Tata Group, Dr Mathai served as minister for railways, and thereafter as finance minister, in the Indian government headed by Prime Minister Jawaharlal Nehru, which is tribute to his intellectual calibre. Post his ministerial stint, he returned to the Tata Group in 1950, as the director-in-charge of Tata Steel, a position he held until his retirement. Overall, he served the Tata Group for fifteen years, a stint that he termed 'the period of my life that I enjoyed most', going on to also say of this tenure—'It was a pleasure to work with people who combined zest for work with a sense of humour.'

Sumant Moolgaokar: The Tata Group's formidable presence in the automobiles sector was shaped over four decades by a very bright and totally committed engineer, Sumant Moolgaokar. Having completed his engineering studies at Pune and London, Moolgaokar joined J.R.D. Tata's leadership team and created the enterprise which has made the Tata name, on four wheels, so ubiquitous on the roads of India. He drove standards of world-class excellence in everything that he touched, and famously said, 'Do not accept second-rate work. Accept the best, and ask for it. Pursue it relentlessly and you will get it.' The Tata Sumo vehicle was named after him, combining the first two alphabets each, of his first and last names.

Rustomji Homusji or 'Russi' Mody: Russi Mody was not an engineer by any stretch of imagination, but he nonetheless led one of India's largest manufacturing companies, Tata Steel, with great distinction for several years. Mody joined the Tata Group in 1939 as an office assistant in Tata Steel and rose to become managing director more than three decades later and eventually succeeded J.R.D. Tata as the chairman of Tata Steel in 1984. A maverick with a large heart and an equally large appetite for life, his outstanding human relations skills are the stuff of legend, in Jamshedpur and elsewhere. He nurtured exceptionally good talent, took exemplary care of employees and it is said that he personally knew the names of several thousand workers in the Tata Steel plant.

Darbari Seth: A technocrat at his core, Darbari Seth joined the Tata Group as a young chemical engineer in 1939. Seth retired from the group as a director of Tata Sons and chairman of several companies more than fifty years later, in 1994. Braving several challenges at Mithapur (the city of salt), he created the chemicals business of the Tata Group. Interestingly, he went on to create two popular consumer brands, Tata Salt and Tata Tea, which are market leaders in their segments and are consumed by approximately half the population of India today.

Nani Palkhivala: Eminent jurist, legal luminary, tax expert and economist, Nani Palkhivala is best known for being a great defender of the Indian Constitution, and a vocal advocate of free enterprise. He was also a doyen of the Tata Group, worked closely with J.R.D. Tata and served on the boards of companies such as Tata Steel, Tata Motors, Associated Cement Companies (ACC) and the Taj Group of Hotels for several years. As the legal advisor to the Tatas, and director of Tata Sons, he brought to bear one of the sharpest brains of modern times on a range of corporate issues. Interestingly, his legendary speeches on the Indian budget, delivered for several years to packed audiences in large stadiums in Mumbai, were also crafted in his fourth-floor corner office in the Tata Group headquarters, Bombay House.

F.C. Kohli: Fakir Chand Kohli migrated from Pakistan to India, following the partition of the country at the time of Independence. He completed his studies in electrical engineering at the Massachusetts Institute of Technology in the US, returned to India in 1951 and joined the Tata electric companies. In 1969, he became the general manager of Tata Consultancy Services, which had just been created as a computers and information technology division of Tata Sons. He led Tata Consultancy Services as its founder CEO, thus creating what is today the finest and largest IT services company in the country. He is often referred to as the father of the Indian software industry and the Tata Group has been his professional home for an amazing sixty-five years. In 2018, FCK is still a sprightly ninety-four-year-old, is seen at many Tata events, speaks with a twinkle in his eye and walks with a spring in his step.

Xerxes Desai: Xerxes Desai created Titan, a company of the Tata Group that has transformed three lifestyle industries in India—wrist watches, jewellery and eyewear—and has its eye on many more. He joined the Tata Administrative Services (TAS) in 1963 and served the Tata Group until his retirement in 2002. The TAS is a central management cadre, created by J.R.D. Tata in 1956, to nurture fine, well-rounded professionals in the Tata Group. It continues to be one of the top-ranked career options amongst students graduating from the best business schools in India today and has provided many outstanding leaders to the Tatas in the modern era. Xerxes Desai is a very good example as a brilliant visionary and leader, lover of great design, astute marketer, perfectionist, dedicated to the community and yet a maverick at heart. He represents the sort of professional that can power the future of Tata Group.

There are many more stories, of equally outstanding professional managers who have contributed splendidly, over long and distinguished stints, to the Tata saga. Names like Ardershir Dalal, A.D. Shroff, J.J. Bhabha, S.A. Sabawala, Noshir Soonawala, Ajit Kerkar, R.K. Krishna Kumar, J.J. Irani, S. Ramadorai, R. Gopalakrishnan and Ishaat Hussain come readily to mind. And, in addition, there are my senior colleagues, several accomplished professionals, who are leading companies of the Tata Group today. I hope I can soon write a book where I can narrate the inspiring stories of many of these leaders, because their tales can, I think, inspire a new generation of leaders, both within the Tata Group and outside.

For now, however, I will request the reader to pause here, and consider the profiles of the ten professionals which I have outlined above. From Charles Perin who engaged with the Tatas in 1902, to Xerxes Desai who retired in 2002, is a very long period of exactly one hundred years. Consider the amazing diversity of these extraordinary people—metallurgist, architect, aviator, engineer, jurist, economist, marketer—who have all been inspired to work for the Tatas. They have helped create this great Institution, relentlessly building it brick by brick, over the decades.

The Tatas have constantly drawn from a deep and diverse well of talent, and have then provided an exemplary platform for such talent to blossom. There has been an abiding recognition that professional excellence, anchored in the right values, is essential for sustained growth. These leaders have, in turn, ably supported their respective chairmen in charting the future, and pursuing the vision set out by the founder, Jamsetji Tata. Quite fittingly, this voyage has now reached an admirable new milestone—in 2017, just a year before the group marked its 150th anniversary, an outstanding professional,

N. Chandrasekaran, who joined Tata Consultancy Services in 1987, has been appointed chairman of the Tata Group.

In this book, you will read many stories drawn from the Tata saga—of chairmen, professionals, and the splendid institutions they have created. You will read stories of dreams, achievements, errors, turnarounds, determination, grit and resilience. You will discover a vibrant, living institution that does not claim to be perfect, but has always demonstrated steadfast purpose. I hope these stories inspire you in many different ways. And perhaps these stories will give you a glimpse of the spirit of Tata, of the fire that burnt in Jamsetji Tata's eyes 150 years ago and which continues to burn bright until this day.

Mumbai, September 2018

Harish Bhat
Author of *Tata Log*

Part I

Leaders

Chapter 1

Ratan Tata

Close Bonds

Ratan was born in Bombay to Soonoo and Naval Hormusji Tata on December 28, 1937. He was their first child, Jimmy following two years later. An old family with old wealth, as a kid, Ratan squirmed when their British driver dropped him off at the all-boys Campion School in the family Rolls-Royce. From childhood, he was uneasy with the ostentatious display of wealth. Even now, he prefers a simple lifestyle with walks on the beach to cocktails at the Taj.

Naval was born with a famous surname and not much else. Distantly related to India's richest and most powerful business family, his parents died early, leaving Naval to be raised in an orphanage. He was thirteen when he was suddenly plucked out of it by the childless and widowed Lady Navajbai Tata, whose husband, Sir Ratan Tata, had promoted some of the group's biggest enterprises.

Lady Navajbai took Naval to live with her in Tata House, near the Bombay Gymkhana, close to the printing presses of the

Times of India. Better known as Tata Palace, it was a residence of epic proportions. Naval's children grew up in splendid rooms of monstrous ostentation with plush velvet drapes, gilt-and-silk sofas and high ceilings embellished with intricate plaster of Paris mouldings.

By all accounts, Ratan's childhood was troubled as Naval and Soonoo did not get along with each other. They finally separated in the mid-'40s when Ratan was about seven and Jimmy was five. The divorce must have left its mark on young minds. Soonoo moved out. Ratan and Jimmy continued to live at Tata Palace, brought up by Lady Navajbai. 'She was like a Dresden doll, always perfectly turned out, often in an exquisitely embroidered *ghara* (a traditional Parsi sari),' says K.A. Divecha, the group's public relations consultant, producing a black and white photograph of Lady Navajbai taken late in life. The grainy texture of the old print can't quite hide the delicate features and flawless complexion. Ratan remembers her affectionately. 'She was a wonderful, wonderful person, of the old world, from whom one learnt a lot, with a very rich experience of life in England and in India. I owe her an enormous amount of gratitude for what she did for me throughout my life. My whole life with her was full of endearment. She had a great influence on my life. She taught me the values which I consider very important in myself.'

From his grandmother, the young Ratan imbibed the importance of dignity, keeping promises and being dependable. Apparently, Lady Navajbai was not only a strong and competent woman, she was also a proud hausfrau, running Tata Palace efficiently and bossing over its retinue of servants. His fondness for his grandmother grew as she made up for the absence of Soonoo in the house. Almost ten years after his divorce from

Soonoo, Naval married a Swiss, Simone in 1955. The next year, Ratan and Jimmy acquired a stepbrother, Noel.

Meanwhile Soonoo had married Sir Jamsetjee Jejeebhoy and had three daughters: Shireen, Deanna and Geeta. Whenever he could, Ratan would spend time with them. On returning from Cornell (he graduated with a BSc degree in architecture with structural engineering in 1962) Ratan moved to Jamshedpur on his first assignment with the Tatas. Six years later when he came back to Bombay, he stayed with Naval and Simone at Tata Palace but moved soon into a bachelor's pad at Colaba. It was small, but it was his own.

The only really close family bonds Ratan had were with his mother and grandmother. Towards Soonoo, he was a devoted son, spending hours at her bedside when she contracted cancer. He was with her when she died in 1982 at New York's Sloan Kettering, a specialist hospital.

Thinking about Soonoo brings a warm glow into Tata's normally shuttered eyes. 'Apart from being my mother, she was a friend. As I grew up, and I was in my late teens, and then early twenties, and going through a lot of soul-searching, she really became a person I could talk to. We shared a lot of our troubles together. We shared a lot of our joys together. We were just very, very good friends. When her house was being rebuilt, she and her daughters came to stay in my flat at my invitation. It was very uncomfortable because it was very overcrowded but for a year they were there. Despite the close quarters and the inconvenience, there was no conflict. It was a very compatible thing and I think that is a very good indication of the fact that if you can do that and not have conflict, you are doing okay.' Ratan designed and oversaw the building of Soonoo's house at Bombay's Pedder Road. It is perhaps the only occasion when his Cornell architectural training was put to use.

After his graduation, Ratan was inclined to stay on in the US. There wasn't much to draw him back to India. He was happily installed in a flat in an apartment complex with a swimming pool in Los Angeles. His Cornell degree easily helped land a job. He could look forward to furthering a career there. Lady Navajbai thought differently and he couldn't say no to her pleadings. He left Los Angeles with an American girlfriend to follow him but she apparently didn't come to India finally.

Tata has never married. In Bombay, he would date on and off, more off than on, and once even got engaged, but broke it off before the cards could be printed. Without a family and children, what motivates him? 'I have asked myself this quite often. I don't have a monetary ownership in the company in which I work and I am not given to propagating the position I am in. I ask myself why am I doing this and I think it is perhaps the challenge. If I had an ideological choice, I would probably want to do something more for the uplift of the people of India. I have a strong desire not to make money but to see happiness created in a place where there isn't.'

A formal invitation from JRD to join the Tatas arrived. Ratan's acceptance letter was becomingly proper: 'Words could never adequately express my sincere gratitude and appreciation for your decision—I shall attempt to express my thanks by serving the firm as best as I can, and to do all I can to make sure that you will not regret your decision.' At this point of time, there was no question of Ratan rising to the top of the Tata tree.

Ratan's first posting was in Bihar and the experience must have been a major challenge after a college lifestyle in the US. In all Ratan would spend six years in the TELCO (Tata Engineering and Locomotive Company) and TISCO (Tata Iron and Steel Company) Jamshedpur complexes. 'Beginning in 1962, I spent six months in TELCO, then was moved to TISCO where I spent two years on the shop floor, then in the engineering division, with projects, and finally as technical assistant to Mr Nanavati, director-in-charge. In those managing agency days that is what the chief executive used to be called,' he recollects.

Ratan's immediate bosses must have sent JRD a good performance report, for Ratan was called to Bombay. He was sent on a short-term assignment to Australia and returned to Bombay a year later. From steel-making, he would later plunge into Bombay's textile industry where he rubbed shoulders with aristocratic mill-owners such as Nusli Wadia and upcoming ones such as Dhirubhai Ambani. The move was a logical transition as Naval was involved in the group's mills, but for Ratan the experience was traumatic. 'I was given two sick companies supposedly to train me. First Nelco and then I had also to take over the ailing Central India Textiles,' Ratan said. 'Central India was turned around, its accumulated losses were wiped out and it paid dividends for several years. Then came the recession in the textile industry and Tata Sons decided not to support the company financially. It was taken into voluntary liquidation.'

The winding up of the group's textile interests didn't dent Tata's reputation as badly as did Nelco's troubled history. 'My first directorship was that of Nelco and the status of that company has forever been held against me,' he says. 'But people forget it is a Rs 200 crore company today.'

The radio and television manufacturer might shine in comparison with R.P. Goenka's troubled Murphy but flickers dully before the tremendous success of newcomers like

Venugopal Dhoot's Videocon or Gulu Mirchandani's Onida. According to Tata, this view represents only one side of the picture. 'It's unfair. No one wanted to see that Nelco did become profitable, that it went from a 2 per cent market share to a 25 per cent market share. Those issues have been forgotten.'

Analysing Nelco's performance in 1982, Ratan said: 'For three years, from 1972 to 1975, Nelco made a profit and wiped out some of its past losses. Then, in 1975, the Emergency came and demand for consumer goods just disappeared, not just for Nelco, but for everybody. At that time the company was poised for growth and we were pumping money into non-consumer goods, which were sucking in a lot of money. This was followed by an industrial relations problem in 1977. So, while demand improved, there was low production. Finally we confronted the unions and, following a strike, we imposed a lock-out for seven months.'

Soon after Ratan's appointment, the subject of Nelco's heavy losses came up at a Tata Sons meeting. The criticism naturally upset Ratan. He had nothing to do with the past performance of the company and he was being penalized for it. 'Jeh came to my rescue,' Ratan recalled, 'and slowly turned round the whole conversation. If you are confident, he will question you and grill you, but if you are fighting with your back to the wall, he will come and duel beside you.'

It was in Nelco that JRD perhaps saw Ratan's determination and supported his plans for the company's growth against the views of many other seniors within the group. When he was put in charge of Nelco in 1971, sales were Rs 30 million, by 1992 they rose to Rs 2 billion with a pre-tax profit of Rs 13.5 million, and in 1995, sales were halved to Rs 1.13 billion though profits were higher at Rs 32 million.

Nelco stiffened Tata's spine. 'I learnt a lot. I don't think I could have learnt as much the hard way as I did in Nelco. I'm most grateful to the powers that be that they gave me Nelco and that they made me fight for three years, wondering where my next payroll was coming from, and to [fight] in a very competitive marketplace. In fact TELCO is the first company in which I could actually do something. In other companies, I was always put in a firefighting situation.'

A Strategic Plan

Ratan had been beavering away anonymously when, in October 1981, the spotlight suddenly swung towards him. He took over the chairmanship of Tata Industries from JRD (then seventy-eight). The move immediately established Ratan as a possible successor to JRD, on par with Nusli Wadia, Russi Mody, Sumant Moolgaokar, Nani Palkhivala, Darbari Seth and a host of others. The announcement sparked wild speculation inside and outside Bombay House. Journalists clambered over each other to interview him. The phone rang itself off the hook. Calmly, Ratan refused to be taken in by the hype. 'The chairmanship of Tata Industries was a titular one,' he says. 'Tata Industries had a great aura about it but it was only a Rs 60 lakh company with no business activity. I had no plan at the start. It was a soul-searching time to begin with.'

Ratan's personal life was in greater turmoil. Soonoo was found to have cancer a few months later. They flew to New York. In the four months in the hospital with her, Ratan wrote out a new agenda for the group called the 1983 Tata Strategic Plan. Later, S.K. Bhattacharya, a leading management consultant, fleshed it out.

It was a plan alien to the then Tata culture. During and after the '70s, the group had become somnolent, its spirit crushed by restrictive government regulations. It couldn't expand. Whatever it produced sold. There was little inclination to improve. Sitting in New York, Ratan worried that too much was being taken for granted: 'There was a need to look into the future and plan for it more than [we had] in the past, and to look at new business areas in a different kind of way.'

He foresaw that India would one day stop being a seller's market and unless the group began a process of strategic planning immediately, it would suffer. While unfolding his plan, Tata explained his philosophy: 'I believe that a lack of strategic planning has a profound effect on the position of a business organization in the marketplace and most of the problems of an organization can usually be traced to lack of planning.'

Keen to change the passive image of the Tata Group, Ratan wanted to propel it to the cutting edge of technology. His argument was that the Tatas have all along been pioneers, taking up frontier industries. Jamsetji Tata set up steel and power plants in the last century when they were unheard of in India. Why should they restrain themselves in the '70s?

'You must remember there was an explosion of new emerging technologies in the West in the late '70s: the super mini and personal computers, driven by microprocessor advances, artificial intelligence, the convergence of computing and communications into information technology and biotechnology. So I thought that the Tatas should be in these areas. We were among the few who would be willing and able to invest in these areas without expecting quick returns, I argued. Why shouldn't the Tatas enter those fields of recent technological advancement which have application potential in India?'

JRD agreed. As he said at the time: 'It would be ideal for the Tatas to get the opportunities to enter high-technology, high-risk industries. In fact, it is almost a duty since only large groups can afford to take risks . . . All industries are going to be high-tech eventually and India cannot afford to miss out on it.' This was all the encouragement Ratan needed to plough ahead.

The hi-tech areas Ratan wanted to concentrate on were telecommunications, oil exploration services, computers and its associated businesses; advanced materials like special alloys and composites; and biotechnology and energy storage systems. Most of these areas were then closed to the private sector. 'However, I felt convinced that these were the areas Tatas must enter as they were the businesses of the future for India. My point was, why should Tatas not be first? As it happened, with the first round of liberalization under Rajiv Gandhi, these were precisely some of the areas that were encouraged. Suddenly our success rate in getting licences was 100 per cent! So next we were running around trying to organize the necessary management and finance.'

The plan, however, failed to win acceptance among some of the senior influential directors for the other business areas, who saw their own interests being subordinated if it were to be implemented. On an academic level, the reasoning made sense. Outlining his viewpoint at the time, Ratan had said: 'Tata Industries, being a collection of chief executives of the Tata companies, offers a chance to be innovative in terms of where the Tatas should be. There is need for strategic planning, looking at opportunities. Such opportunities are available to various companies and there is need to focus them in a central place.'

In practice, however, the directors who had learnt to thrive in a laissez-faire environment within the group, found it difficult to subordinate to the slightest extent their companies' interests for that of the group. Individual companies had done well on their own and any measure which would apparently affect their independence of operations was not one which found ready acceptance.

Recovering from the initial setback, Ratan re-sized the plan to fit his pocket. Nelco's surpluses were minuscule, and Tata Industries' ability to raise funds severely curtailed. He was forced to look at areas requiring little capital investment. Using innovative means, somehow he managed to establish five new enterprises under the Tata Industries umbrella: Tata Honeywell, Tata Telecom, Hitech Drilling, Tata Keltron and Tata Finance. Another four were added later and six more are under implementation. Collectively, these generated Rs 5.87 billion in sales in 1995. Tata Industries thus became the focal point of the group's foray into areas of technology and other emerging businesses.

One of the key features of Ratan's futuristic plan was the division of the group's businesses into eight. These were: metals and associated industries (headed by S.A. Sabavala), engineering (J.E. Talaulicar), chemicals and agro-based industries (Darbari Seth), utilities (K.M. Chinnappa), consumer products (Minoo Mody), services (Freddie Mehta), and hi-tech industries and international business (both under Ratan's charge).

Ratan could not have foreseen that way out in the future he would be in a position to implement most of what he had been unable to do in his earlier years. It started with his appointment as deputy chairman of TELCO, a post which fell into his lap by chance.

Some months before Ratan's appointment as the deputy chairman of TELCO, in July 1988, JRD had finally made up his mind over the succession issue, and his choice fell on Mody. To ensure a smooth transition, JRD drew up an elaborate plan. He was already TISCO chairman. Mody would become TELCO's chairman, taking over from Moolgaokar, its ailing chairman. This would make Mody head of the two biggest companies in the Tata Group, with a combined sales muscle of Rs 30 billion, or a little more than half the group's total sales at the time, and would put him in a strong position to stake a claim to the group chairmanship after JRD retired. In JRD's game plan, once Mody was TELCO's chairman, Ratan would become his deputy.

When JRD played the first move in this grand game of chess, Mody was overjoyed. Had he but restrained his glee, he could have had it all. Instead, Mody allowed himself to prematurely gloat in an interview to the *Business Standard*. His supporters went one step further by crowing about how easily Mody would sort out TELCO's problems. TELCO was then passing through a rough patch with a dip in profits due to its ambitious expansion programme (in March 1987, TELCO made a meagre profit of Rs 29.3 million on sales of Rs 12 billion). Mody's gung-ho attitude alarmed several TELCO executives who began to fear a putsch once he took over.

On hearing the whispers, an incensed Moolgaokar refused to step down. He would carry on in the saddle. He insisted that Ratan should be immediately inducted into TELCO as executive deputy chairman giving him the portfolio of TELCO's day-to-day operations. Palkhivala, then deputy chairman, voluntarily resigned but continued as a director. Mody tried to wriggle out of the tight situation by blaming the faux pas on 'speculative' and 'mischievous' reporting but the damage had been done.

Both Mody and JRD tried to persuade Ratan to resign and publicly state that he would only accept the position under Mody's chairmanship, but he refused to do so. Among the values he had learnt from his grandmother was the sanctity of promises. He would not denigrate Moolgaokar, who had built TELCO over the years.

Mody tried to put a good face on a sticky situation but inside he was seething. News of a strike at TELCO, therefore, may have acted as a soothing balm to his sore spirit.

Corporate Spurs

Trouble at the truck manufacturer's Pune plant had started brewing even before Ratan Tata entered the scene. It gradually developed into one of the bloodiest strikes in recent history. On 7 April 1988, the day Tata was appointed TELCO's deputy chairman, everything appeared normal. By December 1988, when he formally took over the chairmanship from the fragile eighty-two-year-old Sumant Moolgaokar (1906-1989), the tension was palpable.

Nonetheless, few expected the situation to snowball as it did. Most people had their eyes on Russi Mody, wondering how he would react to Ratan's stepping up the ladder leading to JRD's throne. Nobody anticipated that an assault on Ratan's position would come not from an autocratic Tata executive but an unknown trade union leader.

His name was Krishnan Pushparajan Nair, better known as Rajan Nair. The son of a trade union leader and the eldest in a family of eight, Nair worked in Philips before joining

TELCO as a machine miller in September 1976. Six years later he became the general secretary of the TELCO Kamgar Sanghatana (TKS). Though a Keralite, Nair was fluent in Marathi and has been described as a 'first-rate demagogue with a penchant for drama'. In March 1988 he was suspended for allegedly threatening to murder a security guard and sacked a few months later.

The day Nair was sacked, he left TELCO vowing 'to bring the TELCO management to its knees'. He tried his best to keep to his word. The unresolved wage agreement became his rallying point with the management. Nair insisted on Tata's recognition of his status as the workers' leader as a starting point for any negotiation. The management's view was that a dismissed worker with a criminal record could not be accepted as the leader, and while it was willing to talk with other members of the TKS on TELCO rolls, Nair had no locus standi. At the time, there were 8,525 blue-collar workers at the Pune plant and two major unions. From November 1988, antagonism between workers and management worsened. Rumours of a lock-out fuelled the tension. Tata was not new to tackling labour problems, having warded off a sticky situation in his Nelco days. But this was hardly the sort of welcome he needed in TELCO. As a strong believer in the principles of transparency and fairness, he was willing to negotiate, but Nair's ego had the better of him and he thought he could put it across to the new, amiable-looking chairman of the company. He was mistaken. Behind the soft exterior of Tata was a determination toughened by many years of hard experience in the corporate world.

Matters reached a flashpoint on 31 January 1989. Tata's visit to the Pune plant was greeted on the shop floor with a tool-down strike. On the same day, the local authorities saw fit to take Nair into preventive custody. On hearing this, the second shift workers hijacked buses which were supposed to take them to the plant at Pimpri (just outside Pune), and diverted them to the city where they besieged the district court. Nair was released. Tata says that he was unaware of what was happening in the city as he was huddled in a meeting at the plant with Powar, one of Nair's closest aides, and others. 'Nair chose to make out that he was arrested because I said so [but] I didn't get him arrested. It happened totally independently. If there was an issue of getting him arrested, I wouldn't be meeting his people. But that was the last time I met with them because when they went out, they misrepresented the meeting.'

All through the summer and monsoon, the situation inched inexorably towards a strike despite mediation attempts by Sharad Pawar, Maharashtra's chief minister, and others. Nair was not interested in parleying for peace. On 15 March, Nair's men selected about twenty-two managerial personnel and rival unionists and assaulted and stabbed them in various parts of the city. Asked about this, Nair said 'the provocation was from the management because the previous day one of the TKS members was slapped on the shop floor'.

This was as much as Tata could take. From then on his resolve hardened and he refused to give in to any intimidatory tactics of Nair and his men. Meanwhile, Ratan launched measures to build bridges between the management and the workforce. TELCO had been contributing silently to the development of the Pimpri-Chinchwad belt. Now, at the time of its worst industrial crisis, it needed the support of the local community most to correct the impression of the image of the exploitative corporation which Rajan Nair's campaign had sought to project. TELCO shed its conservative image for the first time and utilized the media to create public opinion; the managers initiated a one-to-one contact with the workforce to convince them of the management's intentions and slowly the tide began to turn.

On 19 September, in a shrewd move to woo away support from Nair, the management signed a three-year retrospective agreement with TKS's rival, the TELCO Employees Union (TEC), offering a wage hike of Rs 585 and lump sum arrears of Rs 7,000. There was a stick attached to the tempting carrot. Tata wrote to every TELCO employee in the Pimpri and Chinchwad units, warning that 'the company would have to reconsider its plans for further investments in Pune if the trend of labour unrest continued'. The management claimed that 1,570 workers had accepted the offer and more were expected to follow. Seriously worried, Nair mulled over his options.

Two days later, Nair announced that he and his supporters would go on an indefinite fast at the Shaniwarwada fort. With red bandannas tied round their foreheads, 3,000 or so workers trooped into the fort to begin their fast. Significantly, the initials RNP (for Rajan Nair Panel) and not TKS were printed on the bandannas. Clearly this was not just a management-union issue, but one involving a personal agenda. A one-day bandh was organized in the Pimpri-Chinchwad areas as a display of strength as also to convey the impression of Nair's growing influence in the region. From Bombay, Datta Samant rushed to Pune to express his support.

By the third day, workers were fainting from hunger. At the end of a week, there was a real fear that a fatality could trigger off uncontrollable violence. Pawar stepped up the pressure on both sides to break the deadlock and meet. They agreed.

On the morning of Wednesday, 27 September, Tata flew into Bombay from USA. Nair had arrived from Pune the previous evening. A tripartite meeting between Tata, Nair and Pawar was arranged for the afternoon at Varsha, the chief minister's official residence. Before that, Samant led a morcha to Bombay House while Nair held rallies and press conferences. These vitiated the already charged atmosphere.

In an obvious bid to slight Tata, Nair and his team deliberately arrived very late. Scheduled for 4 p.m., the meeting finally opened at 5.30 p.m. It proved to be inconclusive. Nair was unwilling to concede ground.

Meanwhile, Pawar was becoming increasingly worried about the strike's political repercussions. The Pimpri-Chinchwad area was a crucial vote bank, home to over 2,000 industrial units with an annual turnover of Rs 35 billion and nearly a quarter million workers. Opportunistic politicians of every hue had jumped onto Nair's bandwagon. The Janata Dal leader, Sambhajirao Kakade, was backing Nair. George Fernandes and Madhu Dandavate, socialist leaders, were in constant touch with the strikers. And in the shadow of the Lok Sabha elections scheduled for November 24, Pawar was getting flak from Delhi politicians and Pune industrialists for the state government's kid-glove treatment of Nair. Moreover, TELCO was the largest company in the region and any prolonged dispute would have a tremendous economic fallout. He had to do something.

Under cover of darkness, at 2.30 a.m. on 29 September, the State Reserve and Pune city police launched Operation Crackdown. Eighty buses stopped outside the Shaniwarwada fort's quadrangle. Pouring out of the buses, the police cordoned off the fort, stormed inside, and rounded up the workers.

The evacuation went on in batches until 4 p.m. While the workers were taken to police stations in Pune, a separate vehicle took Nair and his lieutenants to the nearby Ratnagiri jail where they were charged with attempting to commit suicide and defying prohibitory orders. Nair was released on bail the next day but it was clear to everybody that the strike had been effectively smashed.

For Tata, the TELCO crisis became a test of his managerial abilities. Because Nair so obviously lost, the media trumpeted Tata's victory. Tata believed it was a vindication of the principles and values which the group had so zealously protected and propagated all along.

In hindsight, he takes heart from a new spirit of teamwork which emerged during the strike. 'Intimidation led to a hunger strike [but] workers came back to work during the strike. Fearing intimidation, they stayed in the plant. Office staff were manning machines and people in the accounts department were moving materials. Some people were fed up and they came back as an "enough is enough" kind of situation emerged. We started producing vehicles with about 800 people. I think that the kind of spirit that was created in Pune then would never have been created were it not for that conflict. So there were winners. They were caused by circumstances which were, ironically, created by Rajan Nair.

'Today there is a sense of friendliness. I can walk around the shop floor and talk to people. They come and talk to me. We smile and shake hands. I think the union has become a very productive and constructive organ of the company. Perhaps, we took our workers for granted. We assumed that we were doing all that we could for them when probably we were not. We gave a Rajan Nair—or any name—a chance to come and do what he did.'

In Jamshedpur, Russi Mody brooded over the Rajan Nair crisis. Mody was the acknowledged labour expert of the Tata

Group. Under his helm, there hadn't been a single tremor of labour unrest at TISCO for almost half a century. The media's portrayal of Tata as a tough manager capable of handling difficult labour situations posed a subtle threat to the ageing baron.

Indifferent or unaware of the forces around him, Tata concentrated on patching up the shredded labour relations and building up trust between management and workers. 31 March 1991 was a red-letter day. Despite the strike, TELCO overtook TISCO to become India's biggest company in the private sector by sales. TELCO's sales shot up by almost a third to Rs 26 billion and profit before tax grew by 58 per cent to Rs 2.35 billion. Vehicle production rose by 26 per cent to 81,931 units. TISCO's sales were Rs 23.3 billion. TELCO's excellent results established Tata's credentials as a top-notch manager. Reason enough for Mody to feel even more threatened.

Russi Mody

At TISCO, Mody took every opportunity to declare he would leave only when the board kicked him out. Which it summarily did on 19 April 1993, closing a mordant chapter in the group's history. As an outstanding man manager in his heyday with a hands-on style which earned him a Padma Bhushan, Mody had set many precedents. His last was not particularly illustrious. Before this, no Tata chairman had ever been fired, let alone been forced to resign. The sacking came bare days before he was to officially retire on 21 May. It was a pathetic comedown for a rare man who was once the 'toast' of industry.

The bespectacled bon vivant was appointed TISCO's managing director in 1974 and became the chairman in 1984 of India's biggest company in the private sector. His large ego often prompted him to say 'There are only three great men who have come out of Harrow in this century—Jawaharlal Nehru, Winston Churchill and Russi Mody.'

So why did JRD sack a man who once was thought to be one of India's most astute managers? He didn't have a choice: Mody forced it upon himself. He displayed a singular lack of finesse during his last few years with the Tatas. Had he behaved with greater decorum, he could have had a much more graceful exit and assured himself pride of place in Tata history.

The last straw was an interview published in *The Hindu* in which Mody accused Ratan (TISCO's then deputy chairman) and Jamshed J. Irani (its managing director) of mismanaging TISCO's affairs and causing its share prices to crash. He also threatened to launch a campaign to mobilize support for himself from shareholders and financial institutions.

At an emergency meeting on 19 April 1993, there was a great deal of anger and resentment at Mody's statements. As Ratan pointed out, 'The main issue is that a chairman either agrees with his management's policies, or he leaves the board.' Coming as it did after a series of Mody misdemeanours and with tempers running high, it was a foregone conclusion that the board would fire Mody. And when the resolution was put to the vote, it was unanimously passed. Ratan Tata would be 'chairman of the company as from today'.

Earlier, Mody had avoided the 25 March 1991 Tata Sons board meeting which appointed Ratan as chairman of Tata Sons, but the day JRD handed over his crown to Ratan, Mody began to worry in earnest. Tata had become TISCO's deputy chairman on 31 January 1985, and as group chairman would undoubtedly take over TISCO's chairmanship from Mody whenever Mody chose to retire. However his term as managing director was due to expire on 14 June 1993. Mody was anxious that his protégé, Aditya Kashyap, should succeed him. The only hitch was that there was already a number two—Irani.

On the afternoon of 26 November 1991, a circular signed by Mody quietly announced sweeping managerial changes. TISCO would now have four managing directors. In the new pecking order, Irani was demoted from being the joint MD to additional MD, Kashyap moved up from executive director (corporate) to Irani's former position as joint MD, and Ishaat Hussain, the executive director in charge of finance, was designated a deputy MD. Mody continued as chairman and MD. Despite the intentional fuzziness of the designations, Mody's strategy was transparent. He wanted to move up Kashyap and Hussain, both in their mid-forties, and position Kashyap as TISCO's future chairman with Hussain as his number two.

Mody was so confident that his diktat would be obeyed that he flew off to Europe with Kashyap for a month-long holiday the next evening.

In designing his coup, Mody had totally neglected to take Ratan's reaction into account. And Tata was upset. 'In the largest professionally managed corporation in the private sector, when changes in the senior management structure at the board level and/or succession plans are drawn up, then surely it should be a subject for collective decision-making rather than the decision of any single individual,' he stressed.

Pointing out that neither at or after TISCO's 27 November board meeting did Mody make an attempt to get the board's approval or leave room for discussion, Ratan reiterated his stand that 'the board of directors constitute a collection of independent individuals and each one has the right to express his independent judgement without being accused of being pro or anti'.

There were other arguments stacked against Mody. A professionally-run company had to take more than ordinary care not to show favouritism. It was true that the divorced Mody had never hidden the fact that Kashyap was his constant companion and legal heir, yet others on the Tata Steel board were perturbed by the impropriety of the methods adopted to suddenly elevate Kashyap. Mody had overreached himself and had to be curbed. Furthermore, it was not as if Irani lacked experience or was incompetent. On the contrary, the government had once sounded him out for the chairmanship of the Steel Authority of India. Palkhivala and Nusli Wadia endorsed Ratan's hard line. Palkhivala, the group's legal expert, discovered that Mody had violated TISCO's articles of association by not informing the board of the changes prior to sending out the circular.

Mody's friends lost no time in updating him in London, but he failed to fully appreciate the vigour of the forces building up against him in his absence. On 29 December, he flew into Delhi from London where he tried unsuccessfully to meet Narasimha Rao, the prime minister, and Manmohan Singh, the finance minister. On the afternoon of 31 December, Mody arrived in Bombay and drove straight to Bombay House for a private meeting with JRD. Mody also began hectic lobbying of the outside directors, but it was apparent to him that he did not have a case to be backed.

By 2.30 p.m. on 1 January, a compromise had been hammered out. Mody would apologize to the board, Irani would be clearly number two, there would be only two managing directors—Mody and Irani. The rest would be executive directors. The expected discord at the TISCO meeting did not materialize. By 4.55 p.m., the show was over. It was a clear victory for Ratan.

Heroically, Mody wrapped a few tattered shreds of black humour around him. At TISCO's EGM the next day, when a shareholder asked what award Mody should get when *Business India* had named Ratan Businessman of the Year and Irani was Steelman of the Year, Mody promptly quipped: 'I got the Bamboo of the Year.'

From this moment, Mody's star began to set. At about the same time Ratan pushed through with his retirement policy which called for Tata directors to give up their executive powers at sixty-five years and for non-executive chairmen to retire at seventy-five. Framed in the larger interests of the Tata Group to promote succession planning, it affected Mody directly as he was on the verge of turning seventy-five.

Mody started to feel insecure and sounded out whether he would be allowed another five-year term as executive chairman if he resigned as managing director. The response from Bombay House was a firm 'No'.

Mody accepted the no with considerable ill grace and was forced to change his position only after Nusli Wadia told him during the lunch recess that if he did not fall in line, he (Wadia) would personally move a resolution at the board's post-lunch session to sack Mody as managing director. Mody then caved in and a formula was quickly hammered out. Wadia woke up JRD who had been taking a post-lunch nap, and an agreement was reached. When the board reconvened at 2.45 p.m., Mody began by calling for champagne.

According to the agreement, Mody was offered two concessions in view of his past contributions as also his long association with the group. He would remain chairman until

June 1993 and he would retain charge of TISCO's international operations. And TISCO would hold off the Tata Sons policy on the retirement age of Tata chairmen and managing directors for the time being. But far from ending the feud the compromise prolonged the uneasiness within the company. The feuding grew into low-intensity warfare and, predictably, the company's operations suffered. Mody accepted the compromise unwillingly and continued to create problems for Irani in the discharge of his responsibilities as the new managing director.

In March 1993, at the Founder's Day celebrations in Jamshedpur, JRD and Ratan once again brought up the issue of TISCO's acceptance of Tata Sons' retirement policy with Mody. Mody had crossed seventy-five on 17 January 1993. Instead of taking the hint, Mody suggested that the policy, if introduced in TISCO, should exempt present incumbents. His predecessor, JRD, had had a long innings. Why should Mody be deprived of his?

Ratan pointed out that JRD's was a special case when the retirement policy was not in place. It was now important to depersonalize structures and remove subjective elements, such as the granting of extensions, in the tenure of the group's directors. Mody asked for the details of his retirement package in case he agreed to step down. Once he had them, he said, he would finalize things.

By all accounts the severance package was very generous but Mody kept hedging the question of his retirement. During the 11 March board meeting JRD eventually introduced the retirement policy, at which point Mody rose, picked up his papers and walked off saying, 'I declare the meeting closed.' The meeting continued after a few moments of silence, this time presided over by the deputy chairman, Ratan. Badly upset by Mody's walkout, some directors strongly objected to his behaviour. The retirement policy was adopted unanimously. The next issue was, when? The board agreed Mody should retire before the next AGM (which would be held in July) but that he should be allowed to choose and announce the actual date. Mody was lucky to be allowed the choice. Later, when JRD phoned him to communicate the board's decision, Mody preferred to have his severance package approved before he announced the date.

At the next meeting, on 13 April, which Mody avoided by going to Delhi, the protests grew shriller. Mody had taken to vociferously bad-mouthing TISCO's performance in the press and on Doordarshan. The board retaliated by passing a resolution that Mody would have to go by 1 May and not 17 July. It took two and a half hours of debate to come to this decision. When JRD phoned Mody to convey the board's decision, he requested time till 21 May as it was an auspicious day for him. Then came the fatal *Hindu* interview. And the sacking. Ratan's perseverance and commitment to principles had managed to bring down Mody from the high pedestal that he had assumed for himself.

Extracted from *Business Maharajas* by Gita Piramal

Chapter 2

J.R.D. Tata

It was a day in keeping with J.R.D. Tata's mood—lowering cloud and driving, incessant rain—as the car ploughed northwards, headed for Santa Cruz airport. In every way, 1 August 1953 was a terrible day.

It was the day Parliament nationalized nine privately owned airlines and clubbed them into two state-owned corporations: Air India International, India's overseas flag carrier, and Indian Airlines, the domestic carrier. Two of these airlines had been started by JRD. One belonged to G.D. Birla. It was all very well for Birla, thought Tata. He hadn't really wanted to get into the business, if his letter were to be believed. He said he had got into the business because of his son, Basant Kumar. And none of the airlines had been making money of late. Birla probably wasn't feeling too upset that his Bharat Airways was being nationalized. But JRD was grieving.

He'd worked hard to build Tata Airlines, the forerunner of Air India (later Indian Airlines), and then to get Air India International off the ground. He had fought with his back to the wall to keep these two companies out of government control. What did bureaucrats know about how an airline should be run? He did. He'd pioneered the business for India, at the expense of the rest of his business empire. Time and again his executives would tell him, 'Jeh, you're spending too much time on Air India.' Instead of looking at TISCO, TELCO and the fifty other companies which made up the Tata empire, he'd sometimes spent up to half his time on Air India. And now the government was going to snatch his creation from him.

The trips to Delhi, the battles he had fought, had been for nothing. First Rafi Ahmed Kidwai, then Jagjivan Ram—even Jawaharlal Nehru—had deceived him. The entire cabinet had ganged up against him. The only consolation, if there was one, was that Nehru had made sure he wasn't totally cut off from aviation. JRD had been appointed chairman of Air India International and a director of Indian Airlines. And JRD was on his way to the official ceremony.

Tata had seen the writing on the wall almost seven years before the axe fell. He'd even warned G.D. Birla that this might happen some day unless they banded together. Birla, of course, wouldn't listen. He'd written back that there was room for everyone!

From 1946 to 1953 JRD had waged an intense war against nationalization in every possible forum: the International Air Transport Authority (IATA), the local media and international news agencies. He'd lobbied members of Parliament and bureaucrats. He gave evidence to the Air Transport Inquiry Committee. In the process JRD lost a valuable friend. The day the government took away Air India and Air India International from him, the relationship between Jawaharlal Nehru and

J.R.D. Tata was damaged beyond repair. The consequence of the breakdown was much more than the mere loss of friendship between two men. A genuine collaboration between the first Indian prime minister and the head of India's biggest business house could, at worst, have eased the increasing tension between Nehru's administration and business. At best, it might have led to greater dynamism in the industrial sector.

As far as Air India was concerned, Nehru had tried his best to make JRD understand the government's position. He wrote to him some months before the nationalization.

> My dear Jehangir,
> I was very sorry to notice your distress of mind when you came to lunch. You told me that you felt strongly that you had been treated shabbily by the Government of India. Indeed you appeared to think that all this was part of a set policy, pursued through years, just to do injury to your services in order to bring them to such a pass that Government could acquire them cheaply . . .
> I feel I must write to you and try in so far as I can, to remove an impression which I think is totally wrong and is unjust to Government, to me as well as to you . . .
> So far as the Tatas are concerned, you know my own high appreciation of the record of this outstanding firm which has pioneered so many projects. I have not heard at any time adverse comments in regard to the Tatas, although there is plenty of criticism of others here . . . But the charge you made the other day which amounted to a planned conspiracy to suppress private civil aviation and, more particularly, Tata's air services, astounded me . . . As a matter of general policy, we have always thought that transport services of almost all

kinds should be State-owned . . . It was chiefly the lack of finances that prevented us from going ahead . . .

During the last few months, that is since Jagjivan Ram has been Communications Minister, this matter has come up before the Cabinet on several occasions. We examined it thoroughly. We were driven to the conclusion that there was no other way out except to organise them together under the State. I remember that even then stress was laid on the excellence of your services, and more particularly, Air India International. We did not wish to touch Air India International.

We appointed a Committee of the Cabinet to go into the matter. Their report was that it would be difficult in the circumstances to isolate Air India International . . .

I do not want you to carry in your mind the impression you gave me when you came here. We want your help in this and other matters and it is a bad thing to suspect motives and nurse resentment. Coming from an old friend like you, this distresses me greatly.

Nehru's letter to JRD was dated 10 November 1952. The moment it landed on JRD's desk, he cabled back. 'Am sorry if you feel that in my distress I have done injustice to anyone but my only idea was to convey to you frankly my view of the policies and actions of government which have brought about the present situation in the air transport industry . . . If as appears from your letter government have already decided upon the adoption of this scheme I can only deplore that so vital a step should have been taken without giving us a proper hearing.'

Nine months later the government nationalized all private air carriers.

The function at Santa Cruz airport marking the takeover of the airlines was held in pouring rain and was typically officious and unimaginative, the remarks perfunctory, a sign of the times to come.

It was still raining when JRD desolately walked out of the small building to the car waiting for him outside. He would spend the rest of his life looking over the government's shoulder trying to monitor the welfare of his babies.

The 'Frenchy'

Jehangir 'conqueror of the world' Ratan Dadabhoy, eldest son of Sooni and R.D. Tata (1856-1926) was born in Paris, died in Geneva and made his money in India. 'Few addressed him with the full pomposity of the name he was born with,' journalist Bachi Karkaria once said. 'He was simply JRD to the world and Jeh to his friends.'

His father was a distant relative of Jamsetji Nusserwanji Tata (1839–1904), the legendary founder of the group. According to JRD, 'My father had no money at all. In fact he lived in Navsari [in Gujarat]. My father used to tell me that until he was about fifteen or eighteen and came to Bombay, he used to walk barefoot in Navsari. He was of a humble family and yet I don't know how Jamsetji Tata picked him up because Jamsetji Tata made him an associate member[1] right from the start.'

Differences with the main branch of the family led RD to walk out of the group. He was then in his early forties. There were quite a few Parsis in France—such as his old friend Munchersha Godrej for one—and RD left Bombay to start a business with him in precious stones. In Paris, he took

French lessons from a Madame Briere and fell in love with her daughter. They were married in 1902. He was forty-two, she twenty. 'Their marriage created a sensation in Bombay,' writes Rusi M. Lala, the group's official biographer. 'Because R.D. Tata had not only married outside his Parsi community but had also taken the revolutionary step of having his European and Christian wife converted to the Zoroastrian faith. Suzanne Briere became Sooni.' The dust raised by this upheaval refused to settle even by the time JRD died.

Sooni and RD had five children: Sylla Petit, JRD (29 July 1904), Rodabeh Sawhney, Darab, and Jamshed 'Jimmy'. JRD, whose birthday falls on the same day as that of Harshad Mehta and Sanjay Dutt, was born the year J.N. Tata died.

JRD's earliest childhood memory is of being thrashed by his father. 'I was about four and I got a thrashing from my father for having kicked the ayah. When she remonstrated, I said, "I can hit you, kick you because you are poor." So when she repeated it to my mother and my mother told my father, my father quite rightly gave me a thrashing. Never understood how anybody could ever say something like that.'

It was an unusual childhood, nomadic and unsettling. His father was mostly absent and JRD, his brothers and sisters had a permanent address only after they settled down in India when JRD was twenty-one. Except for a holiday home in Hardelot, a summer resort in the south of France, they moved from house to house every few months. JRD's childhood was spent mostly in France, with long interludes in Bombay and a two-year spell in Japan (all of 1917 and a good part of 1918). Whenever his wife and children came to Bombay from Paris, RD rented a house. When the family returned to France, it was generally to a new home. JRD's education was regularly disrupted. Some stability appeared on the horizon when RD rejoined the Tata Group and his financial position improved. He built a house at Ridge Road named Sunita after Sooni and lavishly decorated it with everything French—locks, handles et al. But Sooni didn't get a chance to enjoy it to the full. As usual, RD was in Bombay when he heard she was ill. The day he stepped on board a P&O liner to go and see her in Paris, he received news that she had died.

The children rarely saw their father except during the summer months and it was no different after Sooni's death in 1923. He stayed in France barely a week to complete the necessary formalities. He couldn't have spent much time consoling the grieving children, who by all accounts were devoted to her. Two years later, he would recall the children to India, but by then he himself was sick and dying.

The 'necessary formalities' meant breaking up the family. Leaving the younger children in Grandmother Briere's care, RD sent JRD in October 1923 to a crammer in England. JRD wanted to study engineering at Cambridge, and his English needed brushing up. Getting admission wouldn't be a problem, as Sir Dorab Tata had made a handsome £25,000 donation to Gonville and Caius College some years earlier.

There were many students at the crammer at Southwold, Suffolk, mostly foreigners. 'It was a fairly useful time. I worked. I learnt. I boxed. And on one occasion I froze. It was a bright summer day so all the boys marched off for a swim. With gay abandon I jumped in. But the North Sea even in summer is freezing cold. I thought I would die,' JRD recalled. Called L'Égyptien by his teacher in Paris, JRD was 'Frenchy' in England—and not just because of the latest French racing bike his father brought him.

Just as the course was getting over, conscription was introduced in France. Normally, twenty-year-olds had to stay in the army for two years but the eldest in a family could, if he wished, be released at the end of a year. JRD left for France and was assigned to a regiment called Le Saphis. At the end of the year, he wanted to continue for another six months, but RD summoned him back to Bombay. It was just as well: soon after JRD left for India, the regiment was transferred to Morocco and in a battle there the soldiers were killed to the last man.

The End of Childhood

Though RD didn't bother himself much with the children during their formative years, he redeemed himself by securing a rich future for his eldest son. At the time, JRD wasn't overly impressed: he wasn't at all keen to return to India and would have preferred Cambridge. Later JRD would often say that his lack of higher education gave him 'an inferiority complex'. Nine months after JRD's return, RD died.

It was the summer of 1926. As usual, RD had set sail for his annual vacation in France. He hadn't seen the other children and Granny Briere for a while. On Saturday RD danced with Sylla; when they came home, he complained of not feeling well and collapsed in the toilet. News of the fatal heart attack came to JRD in Jamshedpur, in a telegram from the Bombay office, and he took the first train to Bombay.

At twenty-two, JRD found himself the head of the family. Sylla was twenty-four and yet unmarried. Rodabeh was nineteen, Darab fourteen and Jimmy only ten. JRD still had to find his feet in India. 'Although he was no stranger to India, culturally he was more French than Indian,' writes Lala. 'What is more, he had hardly a trusted relative or friend of RD's he could turn to. The one person JRD could turn to for advice was a solicitor called Dinshaw Daji of Crawford Bailey & Company.'

And given the state in which RD had left his financial affairs, JRD badly needed legal advice. RD had been a cautious manager in Tata Steel, India's biggest private enterprise. During the difficult twenties he refused to distribute dividends to TISCO shareholders. Addressing them in 1925, RD had placated them by saying, 'We are like men building a wall against the sea. It would be the height of folly on our part to give away any part of the cement that is required to make the wall secure for all time.' But in his personal affairs, RD was the exact opposite.

'I remember him for his spendthriftness, no it's a wrong word—generosity,' JRD remembered. 'He was always helping people, giving out money, spending money, building his white elephant, Sunita. I remember father coming home after board meetings and distributing the guineas he was paid to us.'

RD used to earn a princely sum. He could draw up to Rs 2 lakh annually from Tata Sons. (The limit for Sir Dorab and Sir Ratan was Rs 3 lakh). Sir Dorab was careful with his money, RD was not. Worse, RD had allowed his private cotton trading business to run up huge losses. Preoccupied with Tata Steel's difficulties in the mid-twenties, RD had ignored or wasn't aware of the shenanigans going on in his London office. The English manager he had hired speculated on the London Stock Exchange with RD's money. JRD would later discover that his losses were passed on to Tata Ltd and the profits pocketed.

To pay off this and other debts, RD borrowed from Tata Sons and from Sir Dorab personally. On RD's death, the Tata directors decided to write off RD's loans in view of his outstanding service to the firm. Sir Dorab, however, insisted that every penny of his personal loan be paid by RD's family, and this became JRD's first task.

Selling off Sunita to Sir Purshottamdas Thakurdas, a Tata director, JRD moved himself and his family into a suite at the Taj. The house at Ganeshkhind was also sold and later the Hardelot property. All that remained intact were their shares in Tata Sons—a third of the total—and JRD's beloved blue Bugatti, a racing car model without mudguards which he drove rather too fast on the Bombay roads. JRD couldn't rest easy until the debts were paid off and RD's offices in London and the Far East wound up.

'It was a difficult period,' JRD told his biographer, 'because I did not have the background or the experience. The will said that I should get the first Rs 3,000 a month, Darab Rs 2,000 a month, Jimmy Rs 1,000 a month and then what was left should be divided among the five of us. In fact, I would have got, I think, the first Rs 3,000 or Rs 2,500 and nobody would have got anything else at all. But we sorted it out easily. I remember consulting father's old friend Dinshaw Daji. He said, of course you could do what you like if all (brothers and sisters) agree. So we ignored the Will. I decided the family income would be divided equally—1/5th each, including the shares. That was that.'

But, of course, it was not. Years later, in a fit of temper, Darab sold off his shares to Shapoorji Pallonji, a construction magnate. Decades would pass before JRD forgave him for the act.

The second security RD bequeathed on his son was his stake in Tata Sons, the group's managing agency, and a position as a permanent director which brought with it a salary of Rs 750 a month. One of the first things JRD bought for himself once the family's finances had stabilized was a £1,200 plane. He went to London to choose it in May 1929, three months after he had obtained his flying licence. 'No document has ever given me a greater thrill than the little blue and gold certificate delivered to me on 10 February 1929 by the Aero Club of India and Burma,' JRD often said.

It was soon after he'd got his plane that JRD saw an announcement in the London *Times* by the Aga Khan offering a prize of £500 for the first flight from England to India or vice versa by a person of Indian nationality. It had to be a solo flight completed within six weeks from the date of starting. JRD exchanged his French citizenship for an Indian passport and became one of the three entrants to the race. He didn't win, but his attempt made him famous.

After RD's death, responsibility for the three younger children devolved on JRD and Sylla. Fond as he was of Rodabeh, after his mother, Sylla was the biggest influence on JRD. Sylla was 'by far the best of the four members of the Tata family and certainly the bravest', JRD once said of her. She died of cancer in Nice in 1963 after a life lived to the full. A tennis enthusiast, Sylla shared her brother's enthusiasm for flying and was the first woman in Bombay to get a flying licence. 'She was like JRD in many ways,' said a family friend, 'gentle, with flashes of temper.' She married Fali Petit from whom she had two children, and divided her time between Napean Sea Road and the south of France.

Slim and aristocratic, Rodabeh's features were a feminine version of JRD's: a long Parsi nose, arched eyebrows, elfin, pointed chin and sharp eyes. She was a skilled interior decorator—the Sea Lounge at the Taj is her creation. She married Colonel

Leslie Sawhney, an executive with Killick Nixon. Sawhney left the managing agency firm to become JRD's right-hand man.

Meanwhile JRD met and married Thelma ('Thelly') Vicaji in December 1930. Like JRD, Thelly (1909–94) had had an unsettled childhood. Her parents—an English mother and a Parsi father—had separated and she and her sister Kitty lived with their divorced uncle, a lawyer, behind the Taj. For their honeymoon Thelly and JRD chose Darjeeling. 'It enabled us to see Kanchenjunga from close proximity [but] we went to Darjeeling in winter not realising how cold it was,' remembered JRD. Few come to West Bengal's summer capital in December, but the governor of Bengal, Sir Stanley Jackson, decided to spend Christmas there. Both decided to leave Darjeeling on the same day but JRD and Thelly left a little ahead of Jackson.

Their car was asked to pull aside until the governor's car had passed. Waiting and shivering in the freezing cold, JRD decided to protest. The plan was that Thelly would step in front of the governor's car while JRD gave His Excellency a piece of his mind. It worked. As the driver braked, JRD ran to the window and shouted, 'Who the hell do you think you are, keeping five hundred women and children in the cold for hours? You damn fool!' Thelly, who also wanted to give the governor a piece of her mind, moved out of the way. Seeing his way clear, the driver shot off. The story flew round Calcutta, Delhi and Bombay, adding spice as it went.

On their return to Bombay, JRD and Thelly moved into a ground floor apartment in Heliopolis at Colaba. Jimmy and Darab were at boarding school but joined them during school vacations.

Always the odd one out, Jimmy had blue eyes when he was born though they later changed to the same brown as the others. By his late teens, he was a giant of a man with rich blond hair, quite unlike his slimmer brothers. Looking at him, nobody could have imagined he was prematurely born. As mad about flying as JRD, after school, Jimmy left for England to train in a select Air Service Training school. 'Jimmy was an excellent flyer and navigator,' said Bobby Vicaji, Thelly's young cousin, who moved in with JRD after his father, Jack Vicaji, died and who was about the same age as Jimmy.

But JRD expected more. If Jimmy didn't do well in a particular subject, JRD would question and criticize him, rather than congratulate him for doing well in other subjects. A perfectionist himself, JRD set his own standards of excellence and when his brothers didn't or couldn't live up to those expectations, he did not extend the understanding they needed. JRD's desire for Darab to excel affected Darab for the worse, according to Bobby. 'Jimmy was perfectly normal and quietly took his hurt, while Darab, slightly unstable to begin with, became unsure of himself.'

In the summer of 1936, the family spread out. Jimmy left to join his friend Hans in London for a flight to Austria. JRD was in Bombay, Sylla was in the south of France setting up a new home for the Petit family, and Fali Petit with the children was staying in a Paris hotel with Rodabeh. Walking into the hotel one day, Petit handed over a newspaper to Rodabeh. It carried a news item on an Indian called Jamshed Tata who had crashed in Austria. 'I could not believe it,' said Rodabeh. 'Jeh rang me from India to ask "Are you going to Austria to fetch Jimmy?" I said, "Yes," and the next morning I left on the train with the undertakers. I wanted to bring back the coffin not in the train but all the way by car. She retraced the steps to the Père Lachaise cemetery she had taken ten years ago and buried Jimmy next to RD and Sooni.

JRD had been much closer to Jimmy than to Darab. 'Darab was always a somewhat difficult child. Very obstinate,' JRD said once. 'He was very intelligent, but he was weak and had no discipline. As a child he had a violent temper and went into rages. He would walk out of the house and cross the street.' Every year, after school holidays, Darab would solemnly and determinedly announce, 'I am not going back to school,' and Sylla and JRD would have to drag him to the railway station.

After school and college, Darab joined JRD at Bombay House. 'He was a very handsome man, very French,' says Dr Francis Menezes, head of the Tata Management Training Centre at Pune. 'But very hot-headed. The brothers didn't get along very well and JRD was furious with him for selling the shares to Shapoorji Pallonji. There was an incident when a general manager of the Taj died. JRD kept him out of the business after that.' After Leslie Sawhney died suddenly while playing golf in Bombay, Rodabeh went to live with Darab. A few years later, she managed to foster a reconciliation of sorts between her two brothers. Darab died in 1987; Rodabeh a few months after JRD.

Back then, however, if life was tough at home, it was a baptism by fire for JRD in the office.

Temples of Modern India

JRD, now in the prime of his life, found the process of adapting to Congress rule riddled with difficulties. The world around him had completely changed. Independent India was nothing like what he had imagined or expected it to be. Under the Raj, he had known everyone of importance. Even his knights—and the Tata Group bristled with them, from Sir Homy Mody to

Sir Ardeshir Dalal, Sir Nowroji Saklatvala to Sir Jehangir 'Joe' Ghandy—knew everyone worth knowing. There was rarely a year when the viceroy's Executive Council wasn't graced by a Tata executive. There was usually a Tata representative in the Central Legislative Assembly. As Sumant Moolgaokar, the upcoming star of the fifties, once pointed out, with men like Dr John Matthai and Sir Homi Mody at the directors' lunch table, the level of conversation was such that 'you talked of national issues. You felt that Tatas belonged to the nation.'

But JRD had kept aloof from the Congress leadership, unlike G.D. Birla. For a group which depended as much as the Tatas did on government patronage, this was a major lacuna.

Moreover, JRD's differences with Nehru started surfacing around the same time. Before independence, 'Jawaharlal was the heroic knight in armour who awakened in me some of the passion and fire that burned within him. While the love and loyalty I had for him remained undimmed to the end, I soon found myself increasingly out of tune with him once he came to power. He knew I disagreed with most of his economic and international policies,' JRD would write many years later in a collection of his speeches.

On Nehru's side, his basic wariness of businessmen warred with friendship. The Tatas were one of the few business houses to emerge from the post-war tax investigations with their reputation fairly intact, but even so, Nehru's attitude hardened towards his capitalist friend. JRD remembered one particularly sharp exchange of words. 'Nehru told me, "I hate the mention of the very word profit." I replied, "Jawaharlal, I am talking about the need of the public sector making a profit!" Jawaharlal came back: "Never talk to me about the word profit, it is a dirty word."'

Instead of trying to patch up their differences, JRD withdrew into himself. In 1948, Nehru invited JRD as a delegate to the United Nations session in Paris. JRD accepted that year, but turned down the invitation the next year when Nehru repeated it. JRD rationalized his pettishness by saying that there was so much to do in India that time spent listening to speeches was a waste. He used the same excuse when turning down Nehru's request to head Indian Rare Earths, one of the earliest public sector undertakings. Short-sightedly, JRD forgot the public relations implications of these prestigious invitations and the signals his refusals emitted. Later, he wondered whether he had been wrong to spurn these overtures.

The relationship fractured beyond healing after aviation was nationalized in 1953. The loss of Air India and Air India International in 1953 was followed by the loss of the group's insurance business in 1956. There were a few reprieves: at least the Tata power companies escaped when the government nationalized power in 1956. And the TISCO township laid out and maintained with such care remained in Tata hands after the Bihar Land Reforms Act specifically excluded Jamshedpur.

Despite the loss of aviation and insurance, the group's growth during the fifties was impressive. JRD doubled TISCO's capacity and the group started making trucks. The management contract with the Americans in the Tata power companies ended in 1951. Once full control was restored, the group drew up expansion plans for them. These three massive undertakings overshadowed other areas which were actually quite impressive. Like other Indian business houses, JRD suffered from takeover fever and he participated in the dismantling of the British commercial raj.

The group acquired a jumble of managing agency firms, some of which made strategic sense while others were rather opportunistic deals. Among the new entrants to the Tata stables was Forbes Forbes Campbell and Company, an English firm of managing agents looking after auto ancillaries, Bombay Safe Deposit, Gokak Mills and Indian Vegetable Products. In 1954 the Tatas formed a new company called Voltas to take over the Swiss-owned Volkart Brothers, a trading company dealing in dyes and pharmaceuticals. The Tatas acquired a minority interest in Macneill and Barry, one of the oldest and largest British houses in Calcutta, which secured for it a substantial indirect interest in coal. The Tatas also acquired the entire share capital of Sassoon J. David, a large investment company in Bombay. A number of new companies were started during this period. Among them was Tata Fisons, a 50-50 partnership with Fisons. And in keeping with JRD's by-now established habit of promoting unconventional businesses, Lakmé was started in 1952 as a TOMCO subsidiary to make cosmetics.

A Friend in the Ministry

TISCO emerged after the Second World War as one of the world's lowest cost steel producers but with its plant and machinery in poor condition. And profits under the existing price controls were too low to buy new equipment. At TISCO's annual general meeting held on 26 August 1947—eleven days after independence—JRD told shareholders, 'An epoch has ended and another, more glorious one has begun . . . the most crying need of the country today is for production and more production and yet on every hand, we are met with the spectacle of falling production and rising costs.'

The government finally took note of TISCO's plight in 1951. Its profit margins were increased and it received Rs 10 crore out of the Equalization Fund. This enabled TISCO to raise output to 1.3 million tons. A ferromanganese unit was set up at Joda, small furnaces were replaced with large basic open hearth furnaces, and a narrow strip mill was built. But what JRD really wanted to do was to build another TISCO. In his mind, he had never really given up the ideas developed in the mid-thirties for a new steel complex, a modern one with state-of-the-art furnaces and machinery. JRD and his team pored over plans to boost TISCO's production and double production to 2 million tons.

The promptness with which licences and permits were issued took JRD by surprise. He knew that G.D. Birla's applications for a steel plant were getting nowhere, and by the mid-fifties it was clear that the government planned to retain steel in the public sector. Moreover, after the bust-up with Jagjivan Ram over Air India and other incidents, JRD had lost his early admiration for Nehru and his ministers. But T.T. Krishnamachari, the businessman from the south whom Nehru appointed as steel minister in 1955, was different. 'TTK could be arrogant, ill-tempered and undemocratic but he was an extraordinary decision-maker,' said JRD admiringly.

'He was the only really independent and decisive minister I have ever known,' JRD would assess years later to a news magazine. 'Though, in many other ways, he was a terrible man. Very difficult, very authoritarian. Yet, he was the only one who defied Jawaharlal's brand of socialism. I guess that was because he himself was an industrialist. When he was minister of steel, he called us and said: "I want you to double production. Go ahead and double your production at Jamshedpur." He encouraged TELCO when he was minister for industries to go in for truck production. Yes, the man knew his mind and was not sold to those silly notions of socialism that were prevalent at that time. He believed in the way the Tatas were doing business.'

What exactly did JRD mean by that? M.O. Mathai, Nehru's controversial secretary, who got on better with G.D. Birla than with JRD, has a possible explanation. In his autobiography, *My Days with Nehru*, Mathai recounts how TTK not only permitted TISCO's expansion programme but also helped remove a thorn from JRD's side. The thorn in question was a chartered accountant who as TISCO's controller of accounts reported certain irregularities to the finance ministry. 'The Tatas found it prudent to desist from going to court and ultimately entered into a compromise arrangement with the government whereby a sum of Rs 75 lakh was paid,' wrote Mathai. The chartered accountant left TISCO and became a joint secretary in the ministry of production in charge of steel. However, after a separate steel ministry was created with T.T. Krishnamachari as minister, the chartered accountant was transferred out of steel and appointed managing director of a public sector undertaking.

Be that as it may, JRD had bigger issues to worry about. TISCO's licence permitted it to double crude steel production from 1 million tons to 2 million and to hike saleable steel from 1.5 million tons to 2 million. It was clear that to complete a project of this complexity and magnitude within three years and to maintain full production in the existing works would demand an unusual degree of coordinated planning. TISCO's original plant had been built by Americans and JRD's thoughts once more turned to that country.

During a 1945 trip to the US as part of an industrialists' mission, JRD had been impressed by its factories. Delivery times were shorter than in Britain, its factories were intact and products more modern. Once JRD had a licence in hand, TISCO entered into talks with Henry J. Kaiser Corporation of Oakland, California. (This was Kaiser Corporation's second major Indian venture. Edward Kaiser was simultaneously helping Birla set up Hindalco). First orders were placed by March 1956.

To pay for everything, TISCO had to raise Rs 120 crore ($250 million), the largest amount of money it had had to find in its fifty years of existence. Retained earnings and internal resources would take care of one-third of this amount, local borrowings fetched another Rs 15 crore. For its foreign exchange requirements, JRD managed to get a $107.5 million (Rs 52 crore) loan from the International Bank for Reconstruction and Development. As Verrier Elwin proudly said, this, 'the largest industrial loan so far granted by the World Bank and the largest loan ever granted for any purpose in Asia, bears testimony to the financial strength and stability of the Steel Company and the soundness of its expansion plans'.

To raise the balance Rs 13 crore, JRD tapped the Indian capital markets. Morarji Desai was then the finance minister. According to the Tatas, he delayed TISCO's issue as he felt that the Tatas should charge a premium, whereas JRD wanted to bring it out at par. A Rs 100 TISCO share which used to be quoted at Rs 200 had come down to Rs 170. The dividend had come down from 8.25 per cent to 6.80 per cent. Bearing this in mind, JRD felt that a premium wasn't justified.

In a letter to Desai on 23 July 1959, JRD grumbled, 'I hope you will not mind my expressing some surprise that the Government should take such detailed interest and intervene in a matter which involved no important question of policy or principle but only commercial and financial judgement on a simple business issue. Would it be wrong of me to regret the passing of the days when businessmen with a good record of efficiency and integrity could be trusted to make such decisions themselves?' This was not JRD's first scrap with Morarji Desai, nor would it be his last. TISCO's expansion programme was completed in 1958.

Decisions on Wheels

In May 1954, JRD flew to Geneva with J.D. Choksi and Sumant Moolgaokar. Choksi was JRD's legal adviser and one of his closest friends. Moolgaokar was director-in-charge of the Tata Engineering and Locomotive Company.

An engineer from London's City and Guilds College (later known as Imperial College), Moolgaokar (1906–89) was born in Bombay. He began his business career in 1930 as an engineer in a small cement company which became part of Associated Cement Companies (ACC) in 1936. He came to JRD's notice when he managed to commission the much delayed Shahabad cement factory. The turning point in his life came when JRD sent him to Jamshedpur. 'I practically forced Moolgaokar to come,' JRD recalled later. 'I forced Sir Homi Mody who was hesitant to part with him at ACC. I said this is the man, we must have him.'

To Moolgaokar, JRD asked, 'How long are you going to make the glue that sticks the bricks together?' Looking after Tata Locos then was a step down, but Moolgaokar packed his bags. He quickly became one of JRD's blue-eyed boys and by 1949 was director of Tata Industries, ACC and the Cement Agencies Ltd, as well as director-in-charge of Tata Locomotives. JRD appointed him Tata Steel's vice-chairman in 1956, when Russi Mody was still a junior executive. Moolgaokar became TELCO's chairman in 1972 and retained TISCO's vice-chairmanship until 1979. Mody became head of Tata Steel in 1985. There was an element of rivalry between the two powerful men, exacerbated by the tussle between the two companies for the honour of being number one in the private sector.

The Tata Engineering and Locomotive Company had become part of the group when JRD acquired it during the Second World War. It made locomotives for Indian Railways. Towards the early fifties, just as JRD had begun to worry about Tata Loco's dependence on a single customer, he read a report on Daimler-Benz. The German auto giant had recovered from the war's fallout and was interested in locating a partner for commercial vehicles in Asia.

The correspondence JRD had initiated culminated in the May 1954 Geneva meeting between Daimler-Benz executives and JRD's small team composed of Choksi and Moolgaokar. On the agenda was a joint venture to make trucks in India. The Daimler-Benz lawyer had a draft agreement ready which Choksi found one-sided. The talks looked set to break down before they'd begun when the Daimler-Benz chairman took the plunge. He looked at JRD and said, 'You draft the agreement and we'll discuss it.' In that moment of trust a partnership was born. The Tata draft was accepted.

The next hurdle was to obtain a licence from the government. Strictly speaking, the Tatas didn't qualify. 'In 1952, the government decided that it was time to replace its somewhat gut-reaction policy by a more studied and comprehensive approach to the automotive industry,' writes Sanjay Kathuria, a World Bank economist. 'The Tariff Commission of 1953 recommended that only companies with a manufacturing programme should be allowed to continue operations. This meant that only five firms were recognized by the government as manufacturers, i.e., Hindustan Motors, Premier Automobiles, Standard Motor Products of India, Automobile Products of India and Ashok Motors.'

With some trepidation, JRD and Moolgaokar went to see TTK, who, much to their surprise, encouraged them to go ahead. With TTK personally snipping away at red tape, permits and licences weren't a problem. The first Tata truck rolled out on 15 October 1954, less than five months after the meeting in Geneva.

JRD wrote to TTK after he'd left the cabinet, 'How often I think and talk of you and of the days when, thanks to the contrast of the present situation, decisions flowed out of Delhi with, at times, alarming despatch; the part you played in the creation of the TELCO Project and the expansion of the TISCO Project was hardly insignificant, as you modestly suggest. In fact it was decisive, such bold and prompt decision-making [is] unheard of today. There was, at least in whatever ministry you headed, a capacity to make decisions and speed in doing so which astounded me. Things are very different today and the problem is not only to get the decision in time but to get one at all.'

An Afternoon Lockout at TISCO

In the 1957 general elections, the communists won one seat from Jamshedpur. This marked the beginning of their attempts to take over the trade union movement and to wrest control of the Tata Workers' Union. They kicked off their campaign by organizing a conference chaired by Shripad Amrit Dange, founder of the Indian Socialist Labour party, leader of the communist group in the Bombay Legislative Assembly and later in Parliament.

At the conference, it was decided to reactivate the Jamshedpur Mazdoor Union and to win over TISCO workers by obtaining three concessions from the TISCO management. These were: a 25 per cent increase in basic pay, an increase in dearness allowance, and the removal of the recognized union. Dange and his lieutenants found it difficult, however, to break into TISCO. Workers at TELCO, the Tinplate Company of India and Indian Tube proved more susceptible.

Trouble broke out in these three units and as a preemptive move, J.D. Choksi (whom JRD had sent post-haste to Jamshedpur from Bombay) and Michael John together requested the Bihar government to hold conciliation meetings with the Jamshedpur Mazdoor Union. The labour commissioner awarded the workers Rs 45 lakh. This was in addition to the Rs 22 lakh paid out a year earlier, and smacked of appeasement. Dange seized the opportunity and even before the ink was dry, the Jamshedpur Mazdoor Union made new demands. This time it wanted further increases in dearness allowance, revision of basic pay by 25 per cent, reinstatement of discharged employees, and, of course, that the Tata Workers' Union should be derecognized.

They followed this up by taking out a procession on 16 February 1958. The procession was poorly attended, but workers began to report harassment at home, and assaults and threats if they turned up for work. Dange kept up the pressure by calling for a strike from 28 April. The labour commissioner promptly declared it illegal. JRD and Michael John personally appealed to the workers not to support the strike, and employees responded by refusing to cooperate with the Jamshedpur Mazdoor Union. The strike fizzled out.

Unwilling to bow out, the communists escalated the tension. On 12 May, party workers started picketing the gates. Despite the manhandling, over half the workers managed to enter their workplaces. Production for the day was hampered (2,400 tons of pig iron as against the normal 3,100 tons) but TISCO didn't stop. The communists' supporters then turned violent. Over the next four days, they 'gatecrashed into the nerve centres of the plant such as the blast furnaces, coke ovens, transportation department, electrical operations section in order to hamper work,' describes S.N. Pandey, a labour historian. Two workers died.

The situation was explosive, and on 20 May, at 5 p.m., the TISCO management closed down the plant. The management clarified it was not a lockout but a safety measure. Barring 1,380 employees (out of a normal strength of approximately 25,000), all the others were asked to leave the premises. The next day, Jamshedpur Mazdoor supporters became even more violent. Shops were burnt and looted, the army was called in and curfew was imposed. From 22 May onward the management started registering the names of workers willing to work in this dangerous atmosphere. As many as 8,950 men came forward that day. By 28 May, according to a PTI report, there was a stampede to register at the Staff Training Institute. Dange called off the strike.

The 1958 strike clearly shows that the personnel department formed after JRD's 1943 memo was effective. TISCO's experiments in labour relations and labour commitment to production tasks set new standards in Indian industry.

Looking back over that turbulent period, V.G. Gopal, who took over the presidentship of the Tata Workers' Union from

Michael John, and who also played a major role in getting JRD's ideas pushed through the workers' ranks, accepted this assessment. 'The strike in May 1958 was politically motivated and fizzled out after two weeks and after 1958 no strike has taken place,' Gopal once told a local newspaper. 'The code of conduct in TISCO is far superior than what I have experienced in the West. Our workers are much better off in many ways than Western workers. In developed countries the management can hire and fire their employees which they cannot do in Tata Steel. TISCO has better consultation systems than what I have experienced in the West. The success of Tata Steel can be attributed to its industrial relations policy and also its adherence to treating employees as partners.'

Swatantra Party

TISCO's golden anniversary in 1958 should have been cause for celebration, but instead of popping champagne, JRD wrote bitterly to its shareholders, 'In the fifty years of its existence, the steel company has made over 22 million tons of steel, paid Rs 175 crore in wages and bonuses, about Rs 45 crore in dividends, well over Rs 70 crore in taxes and Rs 40 crore into Government's price equalization fund. In the process the Company has saved India hundreds of crores worth of foreign exchange . . . It has provided a living and dynamic answer to the charge that private enterprise cannot "deliver the goods", is only inspired by selfish motives and does not serve the needs of the people.'

JRD was worn out by Nehruvian socialism. He was angry over the government's nationalization spree and its 'dirty' compensatory policies. Fed up of Congress' anti-capitalist rhetoric, he was increasingly frustrated by bureaucrats in Air India International, the steel ministry and other government departments. And, after 1957, he suspected there was worse to come. The Communist Party of India emerged as a major block in Parliament after the 1957 general elections. Angry and humiliated, JRD was ready for change. C. Rajagopalachari caught him in the right frame of mind.

Chakravarti Rajagopalachari (1879–1972), popularly known as Rajaji, was a Congressman and had been leader of the non-cooperation movement in south India, though disagreements with Mahatma Gandhi had led him to stay out of the Quit India movement. A powerful orator, usually dressed in a spotless white *jibba* and white *pancakaccam*, he was twice elected chief minister of Madras (1937–39 and 1952–54), and was also briefly governor of West Bengal. Supportive of industry and commerce, he disagreed with Nehru's nationalization policy and slowly moved away from the Congress.

On 15 May 1961, the Tamil leader asked JRD to back a new party he was planning to launch, the Swatantra. 'While you may exercise your judgement and help the party in power, I respectfully urge that in the interest of good government and parliamentary democracy' JRD and the Tata Group should back 'efforts calculated to build up and bring an opposition party into effective operation.' Rajaji ended hopefully, 'Your decision will serve to give a lead to all others.'

Within the group, Minoo Masani was strongly pro-Swatantra. One of the few who advised JRD not to openly support Rajaji and earn Nehru's displeasure was Naval Tata, cautious as always.

JRD mulled over his response for two months before finally deciding to back the Swatantra Party. On 15 July he wrote back to Rajaji, 'We have also realised the imperative need to ensure that the Communist Party is not the only effective alternative to the Congress Party and that India's political life develops in a truly democratic way around two main opposing Parties, neither of which would be to the extreme Left or the extreme Right. This, in our view, is the *sine qua non* for the survival of democracy.' He assured Rajaji of Tata support and went on to explain that the Tatas would continue to support the Congress—which had given political stability—although this policy might appear to some to be self-defeating.

One reason why JRD took so long to respond to Rajaji's appeal was Nehru. A firm believer in transparency, JRD thought it best that Nehru heard from him rather than anyone else about their intentions. Predictably, Nehru blew up. 'You have no business to do that,' he railed at JRD. Taken aback by Nehru's vehemence—JRD had expected him to be upset but not *that* upset—JRD thought it wise to send a letter explaining his decision which Nehru could read when he was in a calmer frame of mind. Many years later, JRD would have to explain another embarrassing decision to another prime minister—Nehru's daughter, when Nani Palkhivala returned her brief following the declaration of Emergency—and face as furious a response.

In the letter, dated 16 August 1961, JRD started out by reaffirming that the Tatas had not withdrawn their support to the Congress 'even though we may not feel happy about some of the policies of Congress and Government, particularly in the economic field'. He acknowledged that Congress rule had provided stability and unity to the country but pointed out that, 'we have been perturbed by the total absence of any responsible and organized democratic Opposition ... As a result, we have been increasingly worried about the future, however distant, when the strong and outstanding leadership which you have provided may no longer be there. I am one of those who believes that the single party regime under which we have lived since Independence has been up to now a good thing for the country . . . But even you will agree, I think, that if continued, this situation contains the seeds of trouble and risk in the future.'

After outlining the dangers of the Communist party as the only alternative to the Congress, JRD touched on the heart of the dispute. 'The only party which, it seems to us, offers any possibility of developing ultimately into a responsible and democratic Opposition, is the Swatantra Party which, after all, consists mainly of people who have been fostered by the Congress, have spent many years within the Congress and, while conservative in outlook, are not reactionary or communal or extreme rightists.'

JRD ended his emotional letter in a vein reminiscent of Nehru's letter of 10 November 1952 penned on the eve of Air India's nationalization. Nehru had then written, 'It is a bad thing to suspect motives and nurse resentment.' Ten years on, JRD ended the latest addition to their correspondence by saying, 'I am anxious that there should be no misunderstanding in your mind as to our views and motives. My feelings towards you and my personal devotion to you and [your] cause . . . remain unchanged. Please do not take the trouble to reply to this letter. I only seek your understanding.'

Just as JRD could not appreciate Nehru's views on aviation, Nehru couldn't agree with those of JRD on the Swatantra party. 'Although you have asked me specially not to reply to your letter, I am sending you this relatively brief acknowledgement,' Nehru wrote on 18 August. 'You are, of course, completely free to help in any way you like the Swatantra Party. But I do not think that your hope that the Swatantra Party will emerge as a strong Opposition is justified. I think that it will be disappointed at the turn of the next General Elections. It seems to me that it has no roots in the thinking of either the masses of India or the greater part of the intelligentsia. Indeed it seems to me to be cut off from modern thinking even in Europe or America. It is quite remarkably out of date and out of step with events. However, that is just my view.'

Nehru was right. After an undistinguished decade, the Swatantra party fizzled out. But JRD wasn't wrong either. Without a strong opposition to check it, the Congress party thought itself invincible and found it difficult to cope with the idea of not being in power. The 'seeds of trouble' mentioned by JRD sprouted in the form of the Emergency declared by Nehru's daughter eleven years after his death. Ironically, JRD was one of Indira Gandhi's most loyal and vocal supporters during and after the Emergency.

Extracted from *Business Legends* by Gita Piramal

Chapter 3

Jamsetji Tata

In 1858 the British Crown stood forth in name and in fact as the ruler of India. After the failure of the uprising of 1857, a vast subcontinent lay still and submissive. The decades to follow were to mark the high noon of British imperialism. In that period, the geographical expression known as 'India' received two benefits: unification of the country into a stable political entity and a railway system that sought to make the subcontinent a single, viable economic unit. Writing of this period in his *Discovery of India*, Jawaharlal Nehru notes: 'Slowly India recovered from the after-effects of the Revolt of 1857-58. Despite British policy, powerful forces were at work changing India and a new social consciousness was arising. The awakening of India was two-fold: she looked to the West, and, at the same time, she looked to herself and her own past.' Indians began to ask themselves why a foreign power had gained such supremacy over their ancient land. Was it because the culture of the West was superior to their own? Or was it because modern science and technology gave Europe a lead?

A new class of Indians was rising, eager to learn English and to benefit from the study of western ways and methods which Lord Macaulay was offering.

The year that Macaulay left for England, 1839, Jamsetji Nusserwanji Tata was born in a family of Parsi priests in Navsari, Gujarat. At the age of fourteen he came to Bombay, and at seventeen he joined Elphinstone College from which he passed out a couple of years later as a 'Green Scholar', the then equivalent of a graduate. The love for literature and books he then acquired was to last him throughout his life. He was fond of reading Dickens, Thackeray and Mark Twain. After initial trading ventures in the Far East and Europe, he started in 1868—at the age of twenty-nine—a private trading firm with a capital of Rs 21,000.

He and his associates obtained a contract to furnish supplies required by the expeditionary force of General Napier in Abyssinia. The share of the profits was sufficient to launch him on his career in textiles. His earlier visits to Manchester had stimulated his desire to manufacture cotton goods. He bought an old oil mill in Bombay in partnership with a few friends, converted it into a textile mill, managed it himself and within a couple of years made it a going concern. He sold it at a profit two years later. There were, at that time, about a dozen textile mills centred in Bombay, which was known as the 'Cottonpolis' of India. Jamsetji Tata decided to plant his new mill where the cotton came from. He picked on Nagpur in central India, and took advantage of the railway system which had, by that time, moved to the area.

The company he floated in 1874 with a capital of Rs 15 lakh subscribed by his friends and himself, was named The Central India Spinning, Weaving and Manufacturing

Company. On 1 January 1877, the day Queen Victoria was formally proclaimed Empress of India, the Empress Mills was inaugurated. Jamsetji had bought, at a low price, marshy land near the Nagpur railway station and had proceeded to fill it up. A local Marwari banker, asked to subscribe to its shares, refused to back a man who was wasting gold by sinking it into the ground. The gentleman lived to admit that 'Tata had not put gold into the ground but had put in earth and taken out gold.' Jamsetji was to launch another textile mill before he stepped on the scene of history as one of the great builders of modern India.

Jamsetji was a nationalist long before this word had any real significance. He was present, for instance, at the founding of the Indian National Congress in Bombay in 1885, and gave generously to its funds. His nationalism, however, was not narrow. It was, like Tagore's, rooted in his love for humanity, arising out of his passionate love for his own land to which he harnessed the creative forces of his genius. Every day of his life, therefore, became a day of preparation for that time when his country would be in charge of her destiny. When he surveyed the untilled industrial field of India he perceived the benefits it could gain through science and technology. Not only did he grasp the full significance of the industrial revolution of India, but his clear mind spelt out the three basic ingredients to attain it. Steel was the mother of heavy industry. Hydroelectric power was the cheapest energy to be generated. And technical education coupled with research was essential for industrial advance. This may be obvious to us today, but it was not so a century ago to a nation subjugated to a colonial economy. In Jamsetji, India had found a man of ideas with the ability to translate them into reality.

Wisely, he concentrated his energies on implementing these three imperatives of industry. Upon these objectives he brought to bear the resources of his wealth and experience, the prestige of his name, and that rare gift only few can command—the full-hearted devotion of his colleagues.

An English observer, Sir Stanley Reed (later Editor of *The Times of India*) described him as a sturdy figure whose 'voice was sonorous and rather harsh; he conveyed to my mind the impression of the energy and force of a man of action rather than that of an industrial seer.'

His day began fairly early in the morning. At times he went for a short walk along Bombay's seafront and after that would drop in to see his friends. At breakfast he presided at the family table, often joined by relatives and friends. He then read and wrote for a while till he went to office at midday. After office, at 6 p.m. he would go for a drive in his horse carriage—later in his car—or play cards and converse at the Elphinstone Club. On his return he enjoyed his dinner. Good food was one of his two indulgences; the other was a voracious appetite for knowledge, which he constantly fed with reading. The curator of the Calcutta Botanical Museum, an authority on Indian plants, came out of Jamsetji's room one day staggered at his knowledge of botany. 'I learnt several things from him,' said the curator. When an epidemic of bubonic plague was at its height, Jamsetji put aside all else and worked on the history and treatment of different plagues with a view to preventing the spread of infection. One day he had lined up his household staff for inoculation, when Colonel Hormusji Bhabha, Inspector-General of Education for Mysore State, arrived. The bewildered colonel was immediately recruited by Jamsetji as a candidate for inoculation. Every day Jamsetji spent a couple of hours in undisturbed contemplation and reading in his study.

A young Englishman, Norman Redford, who paid several visits to Jamsetji, records that on evening drives in his horse carriage, Jamsetji and his colleagues would talk of schemes, schemes, and more schemes. 'Never,' records Norman Redford, 'did I see Mr Tata impatient or intolerant, nor did I ever see him critical of others' shortcomings.' When Jamsetji died *The Times of India* said that 'he was not a man who cared to bask in the public eye. He disliked public gatherings, he did not care for making speeches, his sturdy strength of character prevented him from fawning on any man however great, for he himself was great in his own way, greater than most people realized. He sought no honour[1] and he claimed no privilege. But the advancement of India and her myriad peoples was with him an abiding passion.' The same paper spoke of Jamsetji's 'quiet, strong, stern, unselfish determination to pursue his calling.'

Jamsetji's mind spanned almost every area of human endeavour though he is remembered for his three great nation-building projects and the famous Taj Mahal Hotel. He was never short of schemes. He had plans to construct a huge circular building where the Prince of Wales Museum stands today in Bombay. He wanted it to house an ice factory that would cool offices in the circular building. This was long before Carrier invented air-conditioning.

Jamsetji not only knew his country well, he knew the world as few other men of his time. In his youth, he had travelled to China and the Far East as well as to Europe and the Middle East. In later years he covered North America. He repeatedly visited Europe and America for industrial exhibitions that first became fashionable in his days. He took advantage of these journeys to study steel plants, coal mines and factories abroad. George Westinghouse encouraged him to visit the Niagara Falls to study hydroelectric generation of power.

Wheresoever he toured, whatever good he saw, he wanted to bring its benefits to his country. He introduced to India foreign trees and plants which he personally cultivated at his estates in Panchgani, Bangalore and Ootacamund. While in France he made a study of the cultivation of the silkworm, and when he visited Japan in 1893 he invited the Japanese to experiment in sericulture in India. He picked Mysore for climatic reasons. The Japanese discovered that silk was once a flourishing industry of that state and that Jamsetji had selected the right place. The silk industry was revived in Mysore. Similarly he chose the Sind area to experiment with the growing of long staple Egyptian cotton. He gave detailed instructions to a number of people on how to grow and experiment but, alas, the experiment was not successful.

He opened a park at Navsari, his home town, to house exotic animals. On one of his last visits he imported a pair of Italian greyhounds and white peacocks for breeding.

The textile mill at Nagpur became Jamsetji's laboratory.

He looked after every little detail of its growth. Here he tried experiments in technology and labour welfare never before attempted in India. To conserve the new company's capital, he purchased in Britain low-priced equipment and, consequently, his yarn turned out to be of inferior quality. He replaced it with the most up-to-date American machinery, ring spindles, till then untried even by the mills of Lancashire. In the future, nothing but the best was to be good enough for him.

The excellence of his new plant was matched by his care for the workers. He installed the first humidifiers and fire-sprinklers in India. In 1886, he instituted a pension fund and, in 1895, began to pay accident compensation. He was decades ahead of his time and miles ahead of his competitors. The Empress Mills experiment showed that not only profits but people mattered to him.

Emboldened by these early successes, he decided in 1886 to buy a mill that had proved to be the graveyard of many reputations. This mill in Bombay had spacious acreage, but the unit itself was ramshackle. At forty-seven, Jamsetji took on the challenge of making a 'sick' mill healthy. Humorously he called it 'my rotten mill', not realizing at the time what a back-breaking task he was taking on. This second unit, called 'Svadeshi Mills' to mark the first beginnings of the Swadeshi movement, was massively supported by Indian shareholders who cheerfully invested in Jamsetji's, by now, rising reputation as an industrialist. But two years later the mills failed to pay a dividend. A shipment to the Far East was rejected. Rumours circulated. Share prices toppled to a fourth of the original. The name 'Tata' was at stake. For the first—but not the last—time, a member of the Tata family risked his personal fortune for saving a public company. Banks refused Jamsetji an overdraft when he offered to pledge his family trust. Jamsetji revoked the trust, liberated his capital, sold some Empress Mills shares and pumped more of his capital into the Svadeshi Mills. As soon as the shareholders learnt of this, the shares firmed up again. By an amazing display of personal energy, and by bringing the best of his staff from the mills at Nagpur, he pitchforked the Svadeshi unit into the top bracket of the textile industry. Within eight years, Svadeshi Mills cloth fetched the highest prices and was in demand in the Far East.

Even as he battled for the survival of his industry, he was not too busy to think of the health of his workers. As polluted water was a cause of illness, he installed a water filtration plant and arranged for sanitary hutments. A grain depot was opened, followed by a dispensary, provident fund and pension schemes. In those early years he also introduced a system of apprenticeship. At that time, of course, there was no academic training in textile technology; so he urged graduates to study books from the mill library.

In the 1880s, it was the practice of all managing agents to charge a commission on production or sales, irrespective of whether the mills made a profit. Jamsetji pioneered the principle that a commission of five per cent to ten per cent would be levied by the managing agents only on profits. Half a century later, the Indian Companies Act of 1937 turned his pioneering principle into the law of the land. One of his early biographers wrote: 'Had he no other title to recognition, his conduct of the mills would suffice.' But much more was to come from his fertile genius. Successful in two textile ventures, his name trusted by the public, contemporaries said that Jamsetji would multiply his wealth by adding to his textile units. He and his staff had the know-how to do so if he so wished. Instead, he chose the unknown path to give India steel, hydroelectric power and technical education of a high order. Something had happened to Jamsetji. The nation had become his business.

In 1902, five years before the site of the steel plant was finally located, he wrote from abroad to his son, Dorab, of what his dream city of steel should look like:

Be sure to lay wide streets planted with shady trees, every other of a quick-growing variety. Be sure that there is plenty of space for lawns and gardens. Reserve large areas for football, hockey and parks. Earmark areas for Hindu temples, Mohammedan mosques and Christian churches.

Jamsetji had seen it all in his mind's eye.

In 1904, three years before the steel plant site was discovered, Jamsetji died at Bad Nauheim in Germany. In his last days, he urged his cousin R.D. Tata and close members of his family to carry forward the work he had started: 'If you cannot make it greater, at least preserve it. Do not let things slide. Go on doing my work and increasing it but if you cannot, do not lose what we have already done.' They not only continued but expanded his work. Others reaped, but he sowed.

Success or failure was not a major issue with Jamsetji. He did what was needed to be done in an environment which was not usually favourable to him. He respected Britain for its liberal traditions but it fell to his lot to fight British imperialism wherever it stunted the industrial growth of his own country. For years he waged a war against the P&O Line which charged excessive freight for Indian exports to the Far East. He started, with Japanese collaboration, a rival shipping line. In the freight war P&O finally offered to carry cotton freight free to the Far East; the exporters failed to support Jamsetji and he had to close the Tata Line. But he did fight.

It was a struggle for his successors to set up a steel plant and get under way the hydroelectric projects. It was also a battle to establish a university of science for which Jamsetji had offered his properties worth Rs 30 lakh—a staggering sum in 1898. The then viceroy, Lord Curzon, was 'rather lukewarm' to this project. But for Jamsetji it was the key to India's modernization.

The British authorities were convinced that students who would pass out from this university of science would not find employment because 'India had no industries'. The Secretary of State wrote to Lord Curzon that as the British had not given the green signal to the university plan, Jamsetji would probably divert some of his endowment to his other projects of steel and hydroelectric power. Some of Jamsetji's close friends too poured cold water on the scheme. A lesser man meeting with such discouragement would have withdrawn the offer. Jamsetji was sore, but so clear was his conviction that he would not abandon the project. He simultaneously proceeded with his steel and hydroelectric projects. For him it was not a case of either/or. At sixty, he knew time was running out, but he had put his hand to the plough and he would not turn back.

What followed was the story of India's leap from the Middle Ages to the threshold of the 20th century.

The Steel Saga

At the age of forty-three in 1882, Jamsetji read a report by a German geologist, Ritter von Schwartz, that the best situated deposits of iron ore were in Chanda District in the Central Provinces, not far from Nagpur where he worked. The area named was Lohara, after the iron ore deposits nearby. In the vicinity, Warora had deposits of coal. Jamsetji is believed to have visited Lohara himself and obtained specimens of Warora coal for testing. He took a consignment of coal with him and had it tested in Germany. The coal was found unsuitable. The mining terms offered by the government were too restrictive and Jamsetji gave up the project. But the idea of giving India a steel plant abided with him.

For the next seventeen years Jamsetji maintained a book of cuttings on minerals available in India. A steady flame burnt in his heart before blast furnaces were to be lit in Jamshedpur. In 1899 the viceroy, Lord Curzon, liberalized the mineral concession policy. The same year, Major R.H. Mahon published a report on the manufacture of iron and steel in India. Mahon said that the time had come to establish an iron and steel works on a considerable scale. He suggested that the Jharia coalfields in eastern India would provide the necessary fuel. For iron ore he suggested Salem district in the South, Chanda district in the Central Provinces, and Bengal.

The next year, Jamsetji was in England seeing the Secretary of State for India, Lord George Hamilton. Hamilton had respect for him. The idea of the steel plant which Jamsetji unfolded sparked the imagination of the British statesman. Jamsetji said he had first thought of the idea as a young man. Now he was sixty and blessed with more than enough for his needs. If he undertook this project it would be for the sake of India. Could he expect the support of the government, he enquired. Hamilton assured him he could and wrote accordingly to Lord Curzon.

Speedily Jamsetji instructed his office in Bombay to obtain prospecting licences, and proceeded to the US himself. He wanted the best technical advice. He studied coking processes at Birmingham, Alabama, visited the world's largest ore market at Cleveland, and in Pittsburgh met the foremost metallurgical consultant, Julian Kennedy. Kennedy warned the enthusiastic though ageing Indian that even preliminary investigations would cost a fortune and there was no guarantee of returns. If, said Kennedy, a thorough scientific survey was made of raw materials and conditions, he would build the plant. He suggested the name of Charles Page Perin as the best man to undertake the survey. To Perin Jamsetji went.

Perin later described his encounter:

I was poring over some accounts in the office when the door opened and a stranger in a strange garb entered. He walked in, leaned over my desk and looked at me fully a minute in silence. Finally, he said in a deep voice, 'Are you Charles Page Perin?' I said, 'Yes'. He stared at me again silently for a long time. Then slowly he said, 'I believe I have found the man I have been looking for. Julian Kennedy has written to you that I am going to build a steel plant in India. I want you to come to India with me, to find suitable iron ore and coking coal and the necessary fluxes. I want you to take charge as my consulting engineer. Mr Kennedy will build the steel plant wherever you advise and I will foot the bill. Will you come to India with me?'

I was dumbfounded, naturally. But you don't know what character and force radiated from Tata's face. And kindliness, too. 'Well,' I said, 'yes, I'd go.' And I did.

Before Perin arrived, he sent his partner Weld to prospect for the raw materials.

Geologist C.M. Weld arrived in April 1903 and set out for exploration with Dorab Tata and a cousin Shapurji Saklatvala, who was elected to the British House of Commons. Chanda district was one of the finest for shikar. The trouble was they were not hunting for tigers but for iron ore. They travelled by bullock-cart. Clean water and food were difficult to obtain, they were often compelled to brew their tea with soda water. As days went by, the immensity of the task they had taken on began to dawn on the prospectors.

Weld was meticulous in his observations. Initially, iron ore and limestone were found but Chanda district was short of the right type of coal. Even the iron ore was in pockets and not in continuous areas. So, sadly, the Chanda scheme was abandoned.

Weld was all set to go home and any businessman other than Jamsetji would have tried to cut his losses on an expensive consultant. But Jamsetji invited him to stay on, and explore for iron ore, coal and fluxes irrespective of location. Weld said that he then realized that Jamsetji was inspired by something far greater than the desire to merely amass a fortune.

The next signal came from an unexpected quarter at the very moment Dorab Tata went to tell the chief commissioner of Chanda district that the Tatas had abandoned the prospecting at Chanda. As the commissioner was out, Dorab Tata aimlessly drifted into the museum opposite the Nagpur Secretariat, to await his return. There he perceived a geological map (in colour) of the Central Provinces. On the map, at Durg district, 140 miles from Nagpur, dark colours indicated heavy deposits of iron ore. To Durg did they repair.

As they climbed on the hills of Dhalli and Rajhara, their footsteps rang with the sound of metal. They were walking on a hill of the finest ore in the world—67 per cent iron. Coking coal and limestone were needed, and, above all, a steady supply of water. But water there was none. So they had to look elsewhere. Their labours were not wasted. Fifty years later those very hills were to furnish the ore needed for the steel plant at Bhilai.

Again the hand of fortune intervened. A letter arrived from an Indian geologist, P.N. Bose, who had originally marked the Durg area for ore. Now working for the Maharaja of Mayurbhanj, he had discovered rich iron ore in the state. It was within range of the Bengal coalfields and the ruler was keen to develop his state. In the wooded hills where elephants roamed and tribal Santhals eked out a precarious existence, the lofty Gorumahisani Hill rose to 3,000 feet. It was a superb storehouse of iron ore later estimated at 35 million tonnes, with an iron content of over 60 per cent. Other neighbouring hills were also rich. All the prospects were pleasing, but where was the water? A reservoir proposed had proved impracticable. The search went on. Early one morning Weld and his assistant, Srinivas Rao, plodded down a dry stream on their horses. It was heavy going through the sand: 'At length we came upon a sight which filled us with joy; a black trap-dike, crossing the river diagonally, and making an almost perfect pick-up weir. It seemed too good to be true.'

Weld and Srinivas Rao clambered up the river bank shouting with excitement. They found themselves close by the village of Sakchi near the meeting point of the two rivers, Kharkai and Subarnarekha ('gold-streaked'), which, together, never run dry. A couple of miles away was the railway station of Kalimati. They had come to the end of their search. Three years earlier Jamsetji had passed away at Bad Nauheim in Germany, but his dream was to outlive him.

Tatas had braved the jungle; now they had to brave the financial world. It was initially suggested that capital for such a large and pioneering project would have to come from the London money market. In 1907, the London market was passing through a bad patch and financiers in London also wanted to exert control if they were to invest.

Some faint-hearted souls said India would not be able to raise the considerable capital. Tatas decided to take the plunge into the Indian market, and issued their prospectus to raise Rs 1.5 crore[2] in ordinary shares, Rs 75 lakh in preference shares, and Rs 7 lakh in deferred, a total of Rs 2.32 crore. From early morning till late at night people besieged Tatas' offices in Bombay and within three weeks 8,000 investors had subscribed. The hidden wealth of India surfaced for her first great industrial adventure. From this amount of Rs 2.32 crore a steel plant of 1 lakh tonnes capacity plus the township was set up.[3]

Jamsetji's company had obtained concessions for iron ore and rail freight, and had taken the risk and the burden of the exploration. All the concessions were turned over to the new Tata Iron and Steel Company for an allotment of Rs 15 lakh worth of shares in the new company and Rs 5.25 lakh out-of-pocket expenses to be reimbursed in cash which Tata Sons put in equity, adding Rs 4.75 lakh of their own money. The total Tata stake was Rs 25 lakh—about 11 per cent of the total capital subscribed.

Between the two rivers, a city had to be planned. As the jungles were cleared, in place of towering trees, steel chimneys arose. At the same time, in another part a township grew.

Though the Maharaja of Mayurbhanj had given highly favourable terms to the Tatas, the local 'kings' of the jungle were less hospitable. Tigers killed two tribal labourers. An elephant driven frantic by the din of dam construction stampeded over a number of huts and flattened them. One night a bear crawled into the hut of the railway superintendent and delivered a cub under his table!

Erecting a plant of this nature in the wilderness was called by contemporaries 'a titanic enterprise'. Communications were slow; machinery was hauled over vast distances from home or abroad; labour had to be trained. There was then no pool of technicians or scientists at home to draw upon.

In the early stages, coal was not of uniform quality; designs of furnaces were found unsatisfactory. Even the German crew for the blast furnace was not up to the mark. Charles Page Perin was summoned again from America.

The chief commissioner for the Indian Railways, Sir Frederick Upcott, had earlier told Perin: 'Do you mean to say that Tatas propose to make steel rails to British specifications? Why, I will undertake to eat every pound of steel rail they succeed in making.'

On 16 February 1912, the first ingot of steel rolled on the lines of the Sakchi plant amidst much rejoicing. During World War I Tatas exported 1,500 miles of steel rails to Mesopotamia. Dorab Tata commented dryly that if Sir Frederick had carried out his undertaking, he would have had 'some slight indigestion.'

In December 1916, a confident chairman of the company was to speak to shareholders of: 'Bumper earnings; production 30 per cent above original design . . . ready and willing markets . . . order book full to bursting.' The success was intoxicating. An ambitious programme was taken in hand to expand the steel capacity by five times. The expansion programme ran into stormy weather. Spiralling post-war prices, transport and labour difficulties completely upset price calculations. It seemed the stars were conspiring to crush the fledgling enterprise. Japan was the largest customer of pig iron. An earthquake struck Japan and prices fell. The faint-hearted reeled under the misfortunes. One director suggested that the government be asked to take over the company. Thereupon R.D. Tata,[4] a cousin and colleague of Jamsetji, sprang to his feet, pounded the table and declared that the day would never come as long as he lived.

One day a telegram came from Jamshedpur that there was not enough money for wages. R.D. Tata and Sir Dorab Tata (who was knighted in 1910) struggled to raise funds. In November 1924, the steel company was on the verge of closing down. Sir Dorab pledged his entire personal fortune of Rs 1 crore, including his wife's jewellery, to obtain a loan of Rs 1 crore from the Imperial Bank of India for a public limited company. It was touch and go whether the firm would survive.

Sir Dorab's readiness to sacrifice was honoured by providence. Soon, the first returns from expanded production came in and gave the company a breather.

Meanwhile, a new threat had arisen from the dumping of foreign steel. Thanks to Motilal Nehru and the Congress Legislative Party, the British government finally consented to impose protective duties on imported steel and paid a bounty on steel rails for three years from 1924.

Throughout this struggle for survival not one worker was retrenched. The shareholders went without a dividend for twelve out of thirteen years. There was a certain vision and spaciousness about the men and the times they lived in.

Just before the first ingot of steel rolled in TISCO in February 1912, R.D. Tata had told the shareholders: 'Like all infants this company will have its infantile ailments, its period of convulsions and teething as well as hours of smiles and caresses. It will be then that your courage and ours will be tested.'

His prophecy was to come true.

In October 1923, also speaking to the shareholders at the time of the great struggle and crippling shortage of money, R.D. Tata told them: 'We are constantly accused by people of wasting money in the town of Jamshedpur. We are asked why it should be necessary to spend so much on housing, sanitation, roads, hospitals and on welfare . . . Gentlemen, people who ask these questions are sadly lacking in imagination. We are not putting up a row of workmen's huts in Jamshedpur—we are building a city.'

And in his last address to the shareholders in June 1925, a year before he died, he said, 'We are like men building a wall against the sea. It would be the height of folly on our part to give away any part of the cement that is required to make the wall secure for all time. That is why we and you have to use this money which we have made firstly to build up this great industry which we are making for India and we should not think of dividends until we have done that. Now let me come from the general to the particular—to this sum of Rs 64 lakh net profit which we have made this year and which we propose to use chiefly to strengthen our wall . . .'

R.D. Tata said about the profit they had made that year (after a couple of difficult years): 'We hold this money in trust for you—but you yourself hold it in trust for the Indian nation which has at great sacrifice given you in the shape of protection more than the whole net profit we have made.'

The upward swing came with World War II in 1939. The value of Tata Steel appreciated. Armoured cars were fitted with bullet-proof plates and rivets made by Tata Steel. They were called 'Tatanagars'. There was such pride when a report came from the Eighth Army in the western desert, that even when a 75 mm shell burst on one side of a 'Tatanagar', the metal plates buckled but were nowhere pierced, and the occupants were all safe.

After World War II, in association with Kaiser engineers of the USA, the plant, which before the war expanded to a million tonnes, was further expanded to two million tonnes.

The mother of heavy industry in India, Tata Steel has spawned many children around herself in Jamshedpur—The Indian Tube Company (now the Tubes Division of Tata Steel), The Indian Cable Company, The Tinplate Company of India,

Indian Steel and Wire Products (started by Sir Indra Singh), Tata-Yodogawa, Tata Robins Fraser, Tata Refractories and the biggest of all, TELCO.

To get the plant moving in those early years took some doing. The general superintendent, T.W. Tutwiler, an American, was a terror. Beneath a ferocious exterior resided a soft heart. He fired people at the slightest provocation but hired them again gladly. He liked no frills. Every Christmas the directors journeyed to Jamshedpur ostensibly for the board meeting, but, it was said, really to please Tutwiler and play with him his favourite game of American poker. Till his last days in Jamshedpur, Tutwiler could never understand how Indians could beat an American at his own card game.

A chemical engineering graduate called Jehangir Ghandy went to Tutwiler for a job. When asked, Ghandy replied he would prefer to work in the laboratory. Tutwiler bawled out that he wanted no 'goddam book learning' and asked him to report at the coke ovens at 6 a.m. the next day. Years later when Ghandy took over as the first Indian general manager, there were not many things he did not know. Not only steel but men were forged at Jamshedpur.

Tutwiler was succeeded by a genial Irishman, John Keenan. Keenan relates the story of a serious accident in the works when a ladle with 75 tonnes of molten metal crashed on the ground with a deafening sound emitting sparks and burning metal. The confused and frenzied shouts of men were heard above the inimical hiss of steam as red-hot metal hit puddles of water.

Keenan could take only three of the injured men in his small car to the hospital. He chose one who seemed to have a better chance than the others to survive and told his helpers to bring him.

The man shook his head in negation. 'Do not take me away,' he said. Turning his head feebly, the Hindu nodded towards the body of a half-burnt Muslim and spoke. '*Hamara bhai ko le jao* [take my brother],' he said clearly. The Hindu who was in pain and in danger of death remembered, not that the Muslim was of a different faith, but that he was his brother.

The company in its own captive mines and collieries, has a task force of 23,000 people, in addition to nearly 55,000 in the works and the township of Jamshedpur, at the Adityapur complex, the bearings plant at Kharagpur, and in the sales offices and stockyards of the marketing division around the country. In 1971, when the coal industry was nationalized the then minister, Mohan Kumaramangalam, left the mines of the company untouched because he wanted nationalized units to 'sharpen' themselves against the more efficiently run Tata collieries.[5]

A memorable day in the life of Tata Steel was the Golden Jubilee when Prime Minister Jawaharlal Nehru came to open the public gardens bequeathed to the city by the steel company. The prime minister was at his best. He gave perspective to the younger people, 'It is very easy for those of us who think in terms of today to belittle what has been done by those who preceded us, not realizing the conditions under which they lived . . . when you have to give the lead in action, in ideas—a lead that does not fit in with the very climate of opinion, that is true courage, physical or mental or spiritual, call it what you like—and it is this type of courage and vision that Jamsetji Tata showed and it is right that we should honour his memory and remember him as one of the big founders of modern India . . . We have our planning commissions but Jamsetji Tata formed himself into some kind of a planning commission and began his own—not a five-year but a much bigger plan.'

Extracted from *The Creation of Wealth: The Tatas from the 19th to the 21st Century* by R.M. Lala

Chapter 4

Sir Dorabji Tata

In many ways, Dorabji is the unsung hero of Tata—a sportsman, statesman and far-sighted leader, who gifted India both the Olympic ideal and a trust foundation that brought hope to many over the years.

Dorabji (or Dorab, as he was generally called) took over as chairman of the Tata Group of companies after his father's passing in 1904. Although Jamsetji has been generally hailed as the visionary, and his son as the man who essentially took his late father's plans through execution, Dorab was much more than a mere lieutenant. He was himself a leader and a true visionary, who took his father's plans and goals and not only brought them to fruition, but, along with his brother Ratan Tata, improved them greatly.

Following in His Father's Footsteps

The eldest son of Jamsetji and Hirabai Tata, Dorab was born in 1859 and grew up primarily in Bombay. He attended proprietary high school and was then sent to England to continue his education with a private tutor. In 1877, he enrolled at Gonville and Caius College, Cambridge. It was here that the eighteen-year-old's love of sports emerged. He won awards in cricket and football and distinguished himself in rowing, running and riding. After two years, he returned to India at his grandfather's request to enrol at St Xavier's College.

After graduating, Dorab became a journalist with the *Bombay Gazette*, but soon fell under the spell of his family's business. In 1884, he left the paper to join Tata's cotton division at Empress Mills, where one of his earliest assignments was to travel to Mysore to explore opportunities for expansion there. Once the viability of growth there was confirmed, Dorab obtained the necessary government approvals with impressive speed.

Jamsetji was eager for his son to meet the highly regarded Dr H.J. Bhabha while he was in Mysore. During their first meeting, Dorab also met Bhabha's young daughter Meherbai, and it is said that he fell in love with her at first sight. The two were married in 1897, when Dorab was thirty-eight and Meherbai just eighteen. The union was a happy one, although the couple had no children.

A Dream Materialized

Back in Bombay, Dorab took the challenge of supporting his father's vision to heart. Working under Jamsetji and then assuming the chairman role upon his father's death in 1904, Dorab laboured tirelessly towards creating a modern iron and steel industry in India. Tata Steel and Tata Power now exist because of Dorab's perseverance and personal involvement in their creation. In addition to founding new companies, Dorab also fostered expansion across the group. He helped to establish three hydroelectric power companies, an oil and soap company, an insurance business and two cement companies, in addition to supporting J.R.D. Tata's aviation unit and investing in the progress of science and medicine through the establishment of the Indian Institute of Science.

He was knighted in the New Year's Honours List in 1910—a recognition of the devotion and courage with which, in furthering his father's projects, he had also served the country. Not that Dorab's tenure as chairman was without critical challenges. Dorab used the post-World War I economic expansion to propel the exponential growth of Tata. This went remarkably well until 1924, when a perfect storm of economic events collided with progress. That year, prices skyrocketed in response to transportation and labour issues in the West. With rising costs came precipitous declines in revenue. On top of this, a massive earthquake that suddenly drove down demand for pig iron hit Tata Steel's largest customer, Japan.

Dorab may not have realized just how bad things were until he received a telegram from Jamshedpur announcing that Tata Steel did not have enough money on hand to pay its employees. Unable to pay wages from corporate funds, Dorab pledged his own wealth and his wife's jewels to qualify for a bank loan, which would allow the company to continue operating. This personal risk-taking proved critical to the survival of Tata Steel. And when revenue began to rise thanks to expanded production, the loan was repaid.

A Passion for Sport

Dorab's passion for sport led him to advocate India's participation in the Olympics as early as 1919, much before the nation had established its own Olympic committee.

He explained his motivation thus:

> Having been educated in my youth in England, I had shared
> in nearly every kind of English athletics and acquired a great
> love for them. On my return to India I conceived the idea
> of introducing a love for such things there. I helped set up,
> with the support of English friends, a High School Athletic
> Association amongst numerous schools of Bombay, in the
> first place for cricket and then for athletics meetings, which
> embraced nearly all the events which form part of the Inter-
> University contests every year in London.[1]

For Dorab, adopting a game also meant adopting European
clothes, rules and notions of order and 'fair play'. Sport became
the playing field where tradition and modernity met, clashed
and fused.

He was elected president of the Deccan Gymkhana, an
athletics meeting which took place in Pune. The Gymkhana
committee wanted to develop their sports programme more in
line with established Indian traditions, but Dorab insisted on
fusing the two cultures.

Dorab found that the competitors were 'all boys of the
peasant class working in the fields and living off poor fare',[2]
with the organizers proposing to run their 100-yard heats
around a bend, without strings, because their sports ground was
very small and the track was part of a rough unrolled grass field.

Other popular events included a long-distance race of over
25 miles, rightly designated as the marathon. The peasants
who participated were used to running barefoot on hard,
macadamized or dirt roads. Despite their lack of training and
the primitive conditions, the first three or four men ran the

distance in fair time. As Dorab observed, their time 'would compare well with the times done in Europe or elsewhere'.[3] In 1919, some of their performances were close to the times clocked in the Olympics.

With hope in his heart, Dorab decided to send three of the runners, at his own expense, to the Antwerp Games of 1920. 'I hoped that with proper training and food under English trainers and coaches they might do credit to India. This proposal fired the ambition of the nationalist element in that city to try and send a complete Olympic team,' he later explained in a letter to the International Olympic Committee president, Count Baillet-Latour, in 1929.

The peasant athletes had little idea of what was required to participate in the Olympics or of the standard of performance essential to qualify for any of the events. For instance, a key member of the Gymkhana, when asked what time he thought was standard for a 100-yard race, replied that it could be anything 'from half a minute to a minute'. He was astounded when told that it was not a matter of minutes but rather of tenths of seconds.

Dorab became president of the fledgling Indian Olympic Council and personally financed the Indian team's participation in the 1924 Games in Paris—where it is reported that his wife, Meherbai Tata, took part in the tennis mixed doubles fixtures. Meherbai was a top tennis player and had won many national level tournaments in the early 1920s.

Dorab saw the value of India having its own team at the Olympics, while it was still under British rule. It was not just a matter of pride, it was an early step towards independence.

He regularly scouted for sporting talent and established training clubs and facilities to develop it. The Willingdon

Sports Club, the Parsi Gymkhana, the High Schools Athletic Association and the Bombay Presidency Olympic Games Association were all initiated by Dorab. Thanks to his involvement, India won the gold medal in hockey at the 1928 Olympics in Amsterdam.

Reinvesting in India

In 1932, nearing the end of his life, and following the loss of his wife to leukaemia, Dorab placed his entire fortune of over Rs 10 million (the equivalent of $64 million in today's times) in trust, to be used 'without any distinction of place, nationality or creed, for the advancement of learning and research, the relief of distress, and other charitable purposes'.[4]

In establishing the Sir Dorab Tata Trust, he said:

> To my father, the acquisition of wealth was only a secondary object in life; it was always subordinate to the constant desire in his heart to improve the industrial and intellectual condition of the people of this country; and the various enterprises which he from time to time undertook in his lifetime had, for their principal object, the advancement of India in these important respects. Kind fate has, however, permitted me to help in bringing to completion his inestimable legacy of service to the country, and it is a matter of the greatest gratification to his sons to have been permitted to carry to fruition the sacred trust which he committed to their charge.[5]

Soon after this, in April of the same year, as a memorial to his wife, he endowed the Lady Tata Memorial Trust with a corpus of Rs 2.5 million (the equivalent of $16 million in today's times) for research into leukaemia. The Lady Meherbai D. Tata Education Trust was formed as a much smaller trust, partly from public donations, for the training of women in hygiene, health and social welfare.

Dorabji died of a heart attack on 3 June 1932, leaving behind a stronger Tata and India, on and off the field.

Extracted from *The Greatest Company in the World?: The Story of TATA* by Peter Casey

Chapter 5

Sir Nowroji Saklatwala

The son of Jamsetji's sister, Nowroji Saklatwala, became the third chairman of the Tata Group after the death of his cousin Sir Dorabji Tata in 1932. He was immediately confronted with the unenviable task of consolidating the company during the global depression of the 1930s. His upbringing and his fascination with the game of cricket gave him the skills to carry the company through this difficult period in a six-year reign that was to see Tata take great social as well as economic strides.

Born in 1875 to Bapuji and Virbaiji Saklatwala, Nowroji, like his first cousin Dorabji, attended St Xavier's College in Bombay. He began his working life as an apprentice in one of the Tata mills, earning a starting salary of Rs 50 a month.

Nowroji was a quick learner, impressing those around him with his work ethic and ability to understand the intricacies of both the cotton products being created and the economics of the industry. His keen intellect saw him promoted to lead the mills department within a few short years.

Even after a long day of working in the mills, Nowroji rarely turned down an invitation to play a game of cricket. In addition to keeping him fit, the game honed him in the important leadership skills of working collaboratively, maintaining morale and compromising when needed.

As his professional star continued to rise within Tata, so did his reputation on the cricket field. Nowroji played first-class cricket for the Parsi team of 1904-05, representing them against the Europeans. However, his workload at Tata soon prevented him from continuing to play as a team member.

In 1917, Nowroji was named chairman of the Bombay Mill-Owners' Association—a sign of the trust and respect the industry had for him. Four years later, he represented Indian employers at the International Labour Conference in Geneva. Nowroji served his industry in many ways, including working as an honorary adviser on virtually any committee that asked him for counsel. His energy and devotion to his work knew no bounds.

During World War I, he was associated with many committees and rendered particularly meritorious service as honorary adviser to the Munitions Board during 1919–21.

Within Tata, Nowroji was also seen as a valuable adviser and team member, putting his Tata colleagues and employees before himself. Although he was comfortable working behind the scenes, offering guidance and leadership, Nowroji was not shy about speaking his mind. That combination of respect, leadership and flexibility brought him into Tata's inner circle, and he worked alongside Dorabji. Because of that close working relationship, no one was surprised when he was approached to succeed Dorabji as chairman upon the latter's death in 1932.

A Leader for the People

Nowroji's leadership style was shaped by his experiences rising through the ranks of the mill workers at Tata. Always concerned for the well-being of his fellow employees, he pushed for benefits that were virtually unheard of during the early 1900s, including an innovative profit-sharing programme.

'For some time, we have been thinking about a method of associating the employees of the company more definitely with its prosperity in good times,'[1] Nowroji is recorded as saying to a Tata official at the time. 'You will be glad to hear that the board shares our views that we ought to show our employees our appreciation of their work when the company can afford to do so. Will you give full publicity to this [profit-sharing scheme] among all employees and let them know that it is the sincere wish of the company as a whole that its employees should share properly in its prosperity.'[2]

Continuing on his reforming crusade, Nowroji instituted higher wages for Tata's lowest-paid workers in 1937 as well as improved conditions for temporary contractors at Tata Steel. Later, he introduced a club and recreation rooms for employees at Tata headquarters in Bombay House, so that workers would have a place to relax and enjoy some fitness activities.

Battling the Great Depression

Taking the helm during the worst global depression ever experienced, Nowroji saw cost-cutting and consolidation as his most urgent task. Doing more with less became the mantra across the board. He focused first on Tata's core businesses: iron and steel, mills, banking and power, and then turned to aid, through consolidation, several Indian cement businesses which were in turmoil. Although Tata was not in the cement business, it recognized that it was nevertheless a major player in Indian growth and construction.

Businessman F.E. Dinshaw had proposed a merger of the companies for the sake of their continued survival, but, unfortunately, he died in 1936, leaving the merger up in the air. Eager to be of assistance, Nowroji stepped in to try and broker the deal. He started by trying to identify the various companies' common interests and then worked through their differences, negotiating an agreement that was acceptable to all. Thanks to his diplomacy, the businesses merged to form Associated Cement Companies—one of Nowroji's proudest accomplishments.

Taking Care of Others

While Nowroji was mainly known as an advocate for Tata workers, his servant leadership extended far beyond Tata's reach. He was instrumental in proposing a cancer institute to serve all of India and directed funds from the Sir Dorabji Tata Trust—of which he was chairman—to that end.

He also devoted himself to turning around the poor financial condition of the Cricket Club of India. His success led to an improved reputation and the hope of longevity for the beleaguered club. Nowroji was actually the first chairman of the club from its inception in 1933 until his death, and was heavily involved in the development and funding of Brabourne Stadium.

A number of honours came to him in recognition of his public service. He was made Justice of the Peace in 1917 and received the Order of the India Empire in 1923. He was knighted in 1933 and was made a Knight Commander of the Order of the British Empire in 1937.

Nowroji died suddenly of a heart attack in France in 1938, just six years after assuming the chairmanship. J.R.D. Tata, son of Ratanji Tata, Jamsetji's first cousin, was elected to succeed him. At thirty-four, he was the youngest chairman of the largest industrial group in India.

Extracted from *The Greatest Company in the World?: The Story of TATA* by Peter Casey

Part II

Professionals

Chapter 6

Russi Mody

A visit to Jamshedpur wouldn't be complete without a mention of Russi Mody, managing director of Tata Steel from 1974 to 1993. Considered a man manager par excellence, his rapport with workers and his concern for their well-being was legendary. An alumnus of Harrow and Oxford, among the finest educational institutions in England, he would sit with workers, call them by their first names, sip cups of tea and eat chapatis with them to build a sense of bonhomie. In 1947, Chairman JRD summoned him to his office in Kolkata and enquired whether it was true that the 15 or 20 men working directly under him were the only ones who had not joined the recently formed Mercantile Employees' Union. Mody agreed, stating that the workers might have been happy with his style of working and did not find the need to join a union. JRD was impressed. To leverage his people skills, he appointed Mody as a labour officer in the newly formed personnel department at Jamshedpur.[1]

In 1955, the Tata Steel coalfields were suffering from very low productivity and incurring an annual loss of

Rs 50 lakh. Mody, then in-charge of the collieries, interacted with workers and their representatives to understand their problems. In a letter to Chairman JRD, he requested for an expenditure of Rs 55 lakh for new roads, electricity in workers' colony, and drinking water supply for the colliery houses. JRD readily agreed, a statesman-like decision for a loss-making unit. The net result was that after the money was spent and workers' confidence gained, there was a stark improvement in productivity and production.[2]

In his years as managing director, Mody held open houses every day from 7 to 9 am at his bungalow in Jamshedpur. Anybody could walk in and talk about anything of personal concern. This practice was eventually instituted for all vice presidents of the company. Abanindra Misra, chairman of Tata Sponge Iron, recalled that Mody started the 'Dialogue Sessions' with the officers of the company. Categorized into junior dialogue and senior dialogue, 3,000 people would come to participate in the dialogue and ask him questions. He would respond with his earthy humour. As for workers, every week, he sat in the Tata Steel plant shops and listened to their grievances. He would even accept written petitions. Workers had faith that Mody would not disappoint them. Whether his reply was 'Yes' or 'No', he sent a personally signed letter to every petition. This amounted to sending out 10,000 letters every year.[3] In 1979, when 10,000 contract workers, incensed by communists, entered the plant threatening destruction unless their demand for being made permanent wasn't immediately met, Mody appealed to Tata Steel workers and a major crisis was averted.[4]

He often said, 'What is man management? That one must behave naturally with any human being.'[5] He was a man-manager almost worshipped by the workers, and enjoyed the adoration of his managers. He gave opportunities to high-performing middle managers by promoting them to senior positions and giving them greater autonomy. During his tenure, the average age of superintendents reduced from 54 years to 35 years.[6] N.K. Sharan, former chief of sales and marketing at Tata Steel, recalled an incident in the 1980s. For long years, most of the superintendents were coming to work on motorbikes. One became a superintendent after 20 years of experience on the shop floor. In one town hall meeting, Mody shared that a lot of people in Bombay and Delhi were now driving cars. 'I think the time has come, when I would like to see all our superintendents coming in cars,' he announced. Within a month, one could see hundreds of Maruti 800 vehicles across Jamshedpur. 'He got them for all the superintendents, and I could see the transformation in the quality of life of the senior people in one stroke,' reminisced Sharan.

A humorous anecdote has done its rounds several decades since 1973, when the name of the lane on which Bombay House is located (in Mumbai) was changed from Bruce Street. Hearsay has it that Russi Mody was once pulled up by a policeman as he tried to park his car on the narrow road, and reproached with: '*Tumhara baap ka rasta hain kya* [Does this street belong to your father]?'[7] The pompous Mody gleefully showed the name on the street. It read 'Sir Homi Mody Street'.[8] Sir Homi was his illustrious father, a former governor of Uttar Pradesh, and a director at Tata Sons who had mentored JRD in his formative years.

In 1972, the Bihar Government took possession of the Jamshedpur township calling it a 'zamindari'.[9] Though, Bokaro, the public-sector steel plant, 150 kilometres away, was considered an 'industrial estate'. Despite this, Tata Steel continued to bear the expenses of maintaining all civic amenities in Jamshepdur. In the period of uncertainty that followed, there was marked deterioration in the township's functioning as the issue of ownership was unclear. Eleven years later, the government decided to return the township to the Tatas, thanks to Mody's ceaseless efforts. JRD had given up hope for any reversal in the government's decision. He praised Mody's diplomacy and people skills for this administrative victory.[10]

His popularity with the workers was evident. On his birthday, thousands of workers would pour into his bungalow, garlanding him with marigolds and having him ride an elephant in a procession through Jamshedpur. A bon vivant, he thoroughly enjoyed the warmth he received. In September 1989, when he arrived from Bombay for a celebration of his golden jubilee at Tata Steel, a huge crowd of company officials, town residents and tribal workers had assembled at the tarmac. They had brought with them a unique gift—a 1.7-tonne laddu made in the company canteen![11] Mody's was the longest ever stint of a senior executive at Tata Steel. He had risen the ranks to become the chairman of Tata Steel after starting his career on the shop floor with a monthly salary of just Rs 100.

Extracted from *The Tata Group* by Shashank Shah

Chapter 7

Sumant Moolgaokar

Prakash Telang joined Tata Motors as a Tata Administrative Service manager in 1972. A peer of Professor Kasturi Rangan (my mentor at Harvard Business School) while studying at IIM Ahmedabad, Telang, reminisced about his early years at TELCO (now Tata Motors).[1] We were sitting at the Tata Motors Guest House in Pune, overseeing the picturesque Sumant Sarovar Lake, named in memory of TELCO's legendary leader—Sumant Moolgaokar. A man-made lake containing effluent-treated water, it was envisaged by the late Chairman Moolgaokar way back in the 1960s. Nearly 50 years later, it continued to be a birdwatcher's delight with rare species regularly flocking to its banks. A former chairman of Honda Motor Company often visited the lake for birdwatching. With 150,000 trees planted in the vicinity, the place is a green oasis in Pimpri-Chinchwad—Pune's industrial area. It was envisaged by Moolgaokar himself over half a century ago in the midst of a barren neighbourhood, and ably executed by the late B.D. Sharma, the company's chief horticultural officer.

In those years, no tree could be cut on the factory premises without the chairman's written permission, which he never gave. It had to be transplanted.

With nostalgia writ large on his face, Telang went back to the 1970s. 'Innovation has now become a buzzword,' he said. 'But even in those years, Moolgaokar had started a growth division with the objective of doing something new all the time.' Given the learning opportunities, Telang, then in his 20s, opted to work in that division. 'We were expanding the TELCO plant in Pune and setting up a manufacturing facility for which we needed assembly conveyors, testing machines, furnaces, material and equipment. We used to make most of them in the growth division.' He fondly recollected how Moolgaokar, then Managing Director of TELCO, used to come to the Pune plant on Saturdays and interact with young members of the growth division. The hands-on involvement of the MD enthused the team. 'So young man, what is the new thing that you are going to show me this time?' would be Moolgaokar's regular question to them. That sense of challenge placed before them by the top leader to continuously innovate, ensured a high level of motivation. 'How can we do something which is required for the organization?' was the question topmost in their minds. At the same time, it wasn't innovation at any cost or of any quality. Moolgaokar had an eye for doing everything absolutely correctly. So when the machine piping was not done well or if the wiring was slightly inclined, he would not even look at the machine, and just walk away. 'These are the kinds of standards that he built into us in those formative days. We learnt quite a lot from a leader of his stature,' reminisced Telang, who eventually became the Managing Director of Tata Motors in 2009. 'We didn't call it 'innovation' in those days, but innovativeness has always been a part of the Tata Group's *sanskar* (traditions), its way of thinking,' observed R. Gopalakrishnan, former director at Tata Sons. 'In recent years, we have adopted the global practices associated with encouraging innovation in the group, and these have added more power to the spirit of innovation that has been such an integral part of the Tata way of doing business.'[2]

From the 1990s, let's go to early 1980s. Trucks in India were provided with rugged non-synchronous gearboxes. However, Sumant Moolgaokar, then chairman of TELCO, decided that it was the right time to introduce the much smoother and easy-to-use synchronized gearbox for the convenience of the drivers. In those years, synchronized gearboxes were not available in India. They had to be imported and hence were expensive. The company's management committee was not in favour of importing these. Their concern was that the customers may not pay for an additional feature and the company may have to bear the cost.

The committee made a recommendation to the chairman that he should not insist on this feature. His reply made them reconsider their approach. The sheer vision communicated through that one sentence made them introspect their approach to product development. Moolgaokar told them, 'Has any one of you driven a truck continuously for three days? For a single day?' None of them had. He continued, 'Please drive a truck yourself and you'll realise the reason for my insistence.'

That was the time when customers had to wait for several years to get a product despite making full payment. This was due to the cap on production imposed under the 'licence raj'. Even if no additional features were introduced in the TELCO trucks, their demand would have continued to be high. 'Yet, for Moolgaokar, the drivers' safety and convenience were of prime importance,' emphasized Chandra Prakash Lohiya, former manager at TELCO. Moolgaokar believed that even if the customer was not asking for it, and the competition was not providing it, TELCO must work towards product quality that is beyond customer expectations. So extraordinary was his passion and commitment towards customer satisfaction that advocate Charles J.E. Grundy, Moolgaokar's friend of many years, would often share that even on hunting expeditions in Bastar (interior Madhya Pradesh), if Moolgaokar happened to spot a Tata truck, he would buttonhole the truck driver for first-hand feedback on the performance of the vehicle![3] It was no surprise then that TELCO held 75 per cent market share (Leyland had the remaining) and people were willing to wait for a decade to drive a TELCO truck.

Interestingly, the demand for some of the vehicles launched in those years continued till date. One such truck that completed 30 years of non-stop success on Indian roads was TELCO's 407. In the mid-1980s, prime minister Rajiv Gandhi relaxed controls on the Indian auto industry. This resulted in four leading Japanese automakers collaborating with local partners. This resulted in DCM-Toyota, Eicher-Mitsubishi, Swaraj-Mazda and Alwyn-Nissan. In the thick of competition, TELCO decided to independently manufacture its own version of a small truck (LCV or light commercial vehicle) that was in great demand. Developed as Project Jupiter, under the direct guidance of Moolgaokar, several cross-functional teams gave their very best. Proactive collaboration with several suppliers were forged, and a new product was born in 1986. To make the most of the government's policy that fuel-efficient vehicles would pay half the taxes, the 407 met all the eco-norms of the day and emerged as among the most fuel-efficient vehicles of its time. It was a classic David versus Goliath situation where localisation played a major role. In a price-sensitive business, affordable spare parts are crucial for long-term viability.[4] Along with a rugged product suited for Indian roads, TELCO's service network gave 407 the upper-hand, and it successfully overtook the Japanese quartet. Within a year of its launch, 407 had wiped out all competition from Japanese automobile giants and gained nearly 80 per cent market share. By 2016, when it completed three decades of success on Indian roads, Tata Motors had sold more than 500,000 vehicles of 124 variants and five models of 407 and continued to retain over 75 per cent market share in its category. 'Initially, when we started, we were not sure whether it would survive. But that vehicle pushed the Japanese and their Indian partners out of business. It has been an outstanding success,' admitted Prakash Telang, former managing director of Tata Motors, who was part of Project Jupiter and had seen the three-decade-long successful run of Tata 407.[5]

Extracted from *The Tata Group* by Shashank Shah

Chapter 8

Xerxes Desai

Clara Lobo manages the beautiful Tanishq showroom on Turner Road, a busy high street in the upscale Bandra area of Mumbai. Inside the store, a family is buying gold jewellery for their daughter's wedding in a few weeks' time. A young couple has just walked in to look at engagement rings. Saleswomen, dressed in elegant brown sarees, are navigating the couple through an assortment of styles. At another counter, two women look visibly excited while making a selection of a set of diamond-studded bangles. Soft music plays in the background. Lobo explains to me how the scenario has changed.

All Indian women want to own Tanishq jewellery today. Our brand has connected so well with them. We have the happiest customers in the world. But it was so different when we began, for many years. I joined Tanishq fifteen years ago, in 1997, just a year after the brand had been launched. We would wait for hours together for a single customer to walk in. Often, a whole week would pass by in silence, and we would feel very depressed. Our performance was so poor that sometimes we even heard that this brand would be shut down.

Two thousand kilometres from Lobo's store, in the garden city of Bangalore, sits Xerxes Desai, the man who founded Tanishq. Now retired, he speaks slowly but clearly in his refined Oxford accent.

Yes, for some years there certainly was pressure to hive off this business. There was mixed support from some people in the Tatas. There was also an opinion that the jewellery business could only be run by family jewellers, that it never could be corporatized.

But I was firm in my view, and I said that any such hiving off or closure would happen over my dead body. We saw the huge opportunity, we had belief and we persisted.

Tanishq is the largest and most successful brand of jewellery in India today, serving nearly a million people (mostly women) each year and generating annual revenues of approximately Rs 10,000 crore, making it one of the glittering jewels in the Tata crown. It is a much-celebrated success that is steadily transforming the second-largest consumer sector in the country. In terms of sheer size, only the food industry beats jewellery.

This is the story of Tanishq, the vision and courage that powered it, and how it overcame all its early errors and struggles to set the gold standard for India.

Wristwatches and Jewellery

Titan Industries, the company which launched Tanishq, was founded in 1984 as a joint venture between the Tata Group and the Government of Tamil Nadu. In April 1987, it launched Titan watches in India. Built on the back of quartz technology and a range of fabulous designs, these watches took the market by storm.

Within a few years, Titan had established a formidable market share of more than 50 per cent in the organized market, frequently walking away with awards for superlative marketing. Titan had become a household name in the country. Even the first movement of Mozart's Twenty-Fifth Symphony, which Titan used in much of its advertising, became as popular as Bollywood songs in many Indian households. Given that very few Indians have any interest in Western classical music, this was a spectacular achievement by itself. Here was a brand that could do no wrong.

Desai, a long-time Tata veteran who founded the company and became its first managing director, recalls, 'Titan was doing extraordinarily well in the market. Sales volumes of our watches were jumping far beyond initial expectations. We revelled in our success.'

At that stage, Titan Industries entered the jewellery business for reasons that could be termed unconventional. In 1991 India faced a serious problem when its foreign currency reserves were severely depleted. The Government of India had to pledge several hundred tonnes of gold from its national reserves to help resolve that crisis. It is ironic that a jewellery business that today uses hundreds of tonnes of gold each year was born at that exact moment.

Titan used many imported components in its watches, even as it rapidly ramped up indigenous production, and the cash-strapped government insisted that it earn foreign exchange to fund these imports. The company was therefore on the lookout for a suitable project that could earn foreign currency through exports.

Desai says, with a mischievous smile, 'We looked at several other ventures before we finally chose to make and export jewellery. For instance, a granite business was actively considered for several weeks, before it was dropped. Indian granite was in huge demand those days for making Japanese tombstones. Fortunately for us, that bizarre idea was speedily buried in its own graveyard.'

The reasons for choosing to pursue the jewellery business were quite simple. World over, at the premium end of the market, jewellers were also watchmakers, and vice versa. Both watches and jewellery were objects of exquisite design and personal adornment. The same stores retailed both in Europe and America. And both participated in the same exhibitions worldwide.

So, Titan Industries invested in a factory and the expertise for manufacturing jewellery. The plant was established in Hosur, an industrial town in Tamil Nadu, at a distance of approximately 40 kilometres from Bangalore. It was also in close proximity to the original unit that manufactured wristwatches. Beautifully landscaped and designed, the factory looked as sublime as the jewellery it would make.

Since the objective was to export all this jewellery and earn foreign exchange, the initial designs that were created in this factory were entirely Western and European in their inspiration. European designers were hired to achieve this.

Jewelled watches were also created. However, two things happened soon thereafter that created immediate uncertainty for the viability of the project.

The demand patterns for gold jewellery in Europe and the United States changed dramatically. Due to a global economic downturn, the ostentatious spending of the Thatcher-Reagan era gave way to a new austerity, and women moved towards the more inexpensive steel-and-gold looks. Titan's fine jewellery was just not competitive enough in this new reality. It seemed that the export game was not worth the candle.

With the onset of the 1991 reforms the Indian economy recovered to a remarkable degree a year later. Other industries such as IT built large export surpluses. Imports were freely permitted, and the need to earn foreign exchange through exports disappeared. Suddenly, for Titan, selling jewellery to Europe was no longer essential.

Desai continues:

> So, here we had a big jewellery factory, and no overseas market worth the effort of developing. This was an expensive plant, with expensive people. The European market for gold jewellery had shrunk, demand from those quarters had declined and it no longer made sense to compete in that space. That is when we turned to the Indian market, and thought of Tanishq.

The Birth of Tanishq

Xerxes Desai had also spoken to J.R.D. Tata in the initial exploratory phases, and sought his views on entering the Indian jewellery market. JRD, who was in his final years as chairman of the Tata Group, was almost childishly excited by the prospect, and quite positive in his response.

'There's a very big market in India for jewellery,' JRD said. 'Given our technical skills and reputation, we should be able to do well.'

But JRD left the final decision to the managing director of the company, like he always did. 'He would hardly ever say no,' Desai recalls, 'unless it was something that he felt was not ethically or morally correct. Only then would he tell me: "Xerxes, in the Tatas we don't do it that way."'

Jamshed Bhabha, a senior Tata director on Titan's board, was even more vocal in his support for a jewellery business. He proudly showed Xerxes Desai a picture of his aunt, Lady Meherbai Tata, wife of Sir Dorab Tata, standing next to Queen Mary of England and wearing the monumental Jubilee diamond that weighed an amazing 245 carats (49.07 g). It was sold by the Tata family in the 1930s to Cartier, then on to Harry Winston, who sold it to a French billionaire, who in turn sold it to diamond czar Robert Mouawad, the current owner. Perhaps there was some fond hope that Titan's jewellery business, if it indeed began, would, some day, reclaim this coveted diamond for the Tatas!

While J.R.D. Tata's and Jamshed Bhabha's views were positive, this was not the response from other directors in the Tata Group. There was deep scepticism that jewellery, a trade that flourished in the unorganized sector, could ever be successful in the hands of a corporate body.

Ishaat Hussain, finance director of Tata Sons, has been a member of the board of directors of Titan Industries for more than two decades. He recalls, 'Jewellery stores in India had always worked with the owner/proprietor model, where the owner knows each customer and builds close personal contact with clients and their families. It was difficult to imagine at that time that this model could be corporatized, that it could change so fast.'

Within Titan too, there were several pockets of cynicism, particularly within the prosperous watch business. Why venture into an unknown industry, when Titan watches were performing so splendidly? Wouldn't it make far more sense to strengthen the watches portfolio by adding new brands or markets, which could further enhance its success?

It is in such moments that one's mettle is tested. Desai reflected on these views calmly, and also discussed them with his senior team, but time and again one indisputable fact leapt out at him. The Indian appetite for jewellery was huge—the size of the market exceeded Rs 50,000 crore annually (today, it is closer to three times that size). The opportunity was too enormous to ignore. Titan's proven manufacturing, marketing and design skills, and its Tata parentage, could be leveraged to crack open this market. Yes, it would not be a cakewalk like the watch business had been, but the rewards in time to come were worth the likely struggles of the initial years, as Tanishq sought to change consumer behaviour and loyalty to the 'family jeweller'.

Leaders of nations and large businesses have to often make lonely decisions, and Desai did, encouraged by the enthusiasm of those who led the jewellery project. In 1996, he decided to launch the first retail showroom of Tanishq in India.

Even as he took this call, he may have looked one last time at a colourful painting of a *bindu,* by the famous Indian artist Syed Haider Raza, which hung in the offices of Titan. The bindu is a dot, which is the source of all energy. Xerxes Desai's decision was on the dot, and here the source of his energy was his belief in the Indian consumer.

Naming the Baby

Marketers spend enormous time trying to create a new brand name. They commission quantitative and qualitative consumer research studies. They appoint experts to analyse the subliminal messages that a brand name conveys. They do many other things that supposedly convey scientific rigour in this area.

However, history tells us that the best brand names are often not born in this way. They just need to have a nice, catchy ring to them, an authentic origin and, if possible, a simple meaning as well. The name Tata is a good illustration: it is the family name of the founder of the group. Similarly, the brand name Apple was chosen because Steve Jobs worked in an apple farm one summer and it came before Atari (a competitor) in the phone book.

The name Tanishq, chosen by Desai and acknowledged today as a master stroke by everyone, has a similar history. Here is his own version of the story:

Anil Manchanda [who was leading the jewellery project in the company] was keen on the name Aurum. But this would look like a piece of the periodic table, and no one would really understand it, so we said no. We had previously used the brand name Celeste in the European market, during the early days of jewellery export. But we soon realized that Celeste had already been trademarked by another company.

So, I thought of the word Tanishq. I was clear that the word should possess a feminine and Indian feel to it. It would also be useful for the names of our two promoters to be reflected in the name. So, *ta* stands both for Tata and Tamil Nadu, the promoters of our company. And *nishq* means a piece of jewellery. The name sounded even better when Fali Vakeel of our advertising agency, Lintas, pointed out to me that Tanishq, when sliced differently, is a combination of *tan* (body) and *ishq* (love). These are words which go very well with jewellery.

But what is really interesting is how the name Tanishq jumped into my mind at the very beginning. I am fond of dogs, and I owned a Harlequin Great Dane at that time, called Monishqa. Also, the young daughter of a close friend, whose brains we had picked in the early days when working on Titan's marketing strategy, was named Monisha. So, I used these names often, and I think they triggered Tanishq, which sounds quite similar! When I tossed it around in my mind after that, it sounded very poetic and beautiful.

Marketers may wish to bear this story in mind when they commission research firms to search for brand names.

An Indian Summer

Tanishq was launched in India in 1996, as a brand of precious gem-set (studded) jewellery. Plain gold jewellery was a very small part of the product offering. As Desai mentioned in a speech many years later, the idea was to make Tanishq 'a composite Indian avatar of Cartier, Tiffany, Asprey and even Ernest Jones all rolled into one'.

Bhaskar Bhat, the current managing director of Titan Industries, explains why this choice was made:

Plain gold jewellery offers little opportunity for differentiation (or so we felt at that time). With everyone sourcing from the same pool of *karigars* (artisans), new designs are quickly copied. Also, everyone knows the price of gold. The customer then adds labour and wastage charges, and establishes the base price, leaving the jeweller with no pricing power. You make money by focusing on volumes and faster inventory turns.

Studded jewellery is a different story altogether. Customers don't really know how to accurately value gems. Even with diamonds, where we have a clear evaluation process based on the four Cs of cut, colour, clarity and caratage, it is not easy to peg down a price. There is also the opportunity to be innovative in design, since people are less likely to copy them, given the low volumes. As a result, the jeweller has more price flexibility, and margins are much higher in studded jewellery.

The decision to get primarily into studded jewellery created a constraint because it meant that Tanishq could not offer any significant variety in 22 carat gold to consumers, despite this caratage being the standard in the Indian market. Eighteen carat gold would have to be used to make Tanishq jewellery, since 22 carat gold is too soft to hold diamonds or other gemstones. Simultaneously, there was also an effort to move the market for plain gold jewellery to 18 carat, with the belief that this offering would enable consumers to spread their budgets over larger or more pieces, since 18 carat gold is less expensive than 22 carat gold. It would also benefit customers because 18 carat gold is more scratch-proof and dent-proof.

The company knew that by doing this it was taking on the risk of trying to change long-standing consumer behaviour. Moving consumers from 22 carat gold to 18 carat jewellery was fundamental to the success of this strategy. However, Desai and team were supremely confident. They had successfully transformed the watch market. They were inspired marketers, recognized repeatedly as the best in the land. There was no reason to doubt that they would not do it again.

In July 1996, the first Tanishq showroom opened for business at Cathedral Road in Chennai. The showroom looked like a highly exclusive five-star hotel. Fitted with green marble, low counters, works of art and some show windows, there was very little jewellery on display compared to other Indian jewellery stores. Staff was hired and trained extensively in the art of customer service. An advertisement campaign was launched with a view to create mystery around the brand and also communicate that the showrooms were as precious as the Tanishq jewellery itself. Now the only thing that needed to happen was for customers to walk in. So they waited . . .

The Indian woman remained totally unmoved.

Gold jewellery was not merely a piece of adornment for her; it was her personal wealth, traditionally called *stridhan*. She was not willing to dilute this important aspect of her life by buying 18 carat gold, which was, in her perception, far less valuable than 22 carat gold. In her view, 'less than precious' 18 carat jewellery was eminently unsuitable, particularly for precious occasions such as weddings and Indian festivals. The few women who overcame this adverse perception and stepped into Tanishq showrooms were promptly intimidated by the opulent surroundings and the Western-style jewellery. 'Not for me' was the most common reaction, which did not change even after several months of intense marketing efforts.

With a bang and a thud, the marketers who could do no wrong were brought down to earth. The expensive jewellery factory in Hosur continued to incur losses, because there was little being sold. Tanishq was in distress.

When It Rains, It Pours

During the period 1996 to 2000, even as Tanishq was failing miserably to attract consumers, the parent company, Titan Industries, suffered many other setbacks as well.

The watch business made a foray into Europe, which turned out to be a misadventure. The losses incurred on this account ran into more than Rs 150 crore, which was a huge amount for the company to bear. A relatively new business in table clocks and wall clocks had to be discontinued, because its potential size and profitability were not attractive enough. The clocks bore the stamp of beautiful design, and the few remaining pieces are still sought after by connoisseurs, but the financial returns were completely inadequate. In addition, the company had invested in a joint venture with Timex Watches of USA, which was also running into major financial and operational challenges.

Bhaskar Bhat recalls, 'We were deep in debt. Our initial successes in the watch market had given us an aura of invincibility, which was now peeling away. The media speculated that we would sell the jewellery business. Some reports even said that the Tata Group was very unhappy with our entry into this sector. The going was getting really rough.'

Indeed, there were several frowns and worried faces whenever the future of the jewellery business came up for discussion. It had already lost more than Rs 100 crore. Some observers reckoned that the brand was stuck in no man's land, and there was no light at the end of the tunnel. To make it worse, the company had to bear these huge losses at a time when nothing else seemed to be going well.

Desai also knew that the core watch business was earning much less money than originally planned, which is why the cash required to support the jewellery segment, on which the project and its borrowings were based, was rapidly evaporating. Several debates erupted now on the future of this business. Some of these debates occurred in Bombay House and were also thereafter tabled at the board of directors of Titan.

A protracted and sharply worded correspondence between Desai and Ishaat Hussain (who represented the Tata Group on Titan's board of directors) was typical of this period. Hussain was concerned about the mounting losses, and he took up the matter in no uncertain terms. The exchange of letters appeared to be veering into a deadlock.

Xerxes Desai says:

Ishaat and I were good friends; in fact, my son had worked with him in earlier years. He was doing his job as a man of finance, but I entirely disagreed with his point of view on the jewellery business. I was convinced the business had big potential; perhaps we had made errors in execution leading to the losses, but we could change that around.

There was also a view in some quarters in the Tatas and elsewhere that jewellery was not our core competence. These people said we were a watch company; that is why we were failing so badly in this new venture. But I ask you, if the Tatas had focused only on their core competence, wouldn't we have remained a textiles and trading group for the past century?

It is to the credit of the Tata Group that though there was significant impatience and discomfort with the jewellery business in the offices of Bombay House, they left the final decision to Desai and the board of directors of Titan Industries.

An interview with Ratan Tata, published in *Businessworld* magazine in December 2000, highlights this approach.

The interviewers, Tony Joseph and Radhika Dhawan, ask him if Titan had entered the jewellery business against the wishes of the group, and was then not delivering. Ratan Tata responded, 'You referred to the case of Titan going into the jewellery business, and the GEO's [group executive office's] contrary view on this. Ideally, where is this kind of issue to be discussed and debated? At the boards of these companies.'

He went on to say that the boards of companies had to be more concerned with their businesses than they had been in the past, and that the CEO should take his directions from the board, which is the requisite authority.

Notwithstanding Ratan Tata's viewpoint, pressure mounted on Desai to hive off the jewellery business into a separate company that could be sold, if necessary. This was in essence an exit plan, and the Tata Group appeared to have lost faith in Tanishq. Within Titan Industries, there was indifferent support from many segments in the prosperous watch section, which considered the jewellery business a bottomless and useless sink for funds. However, there was strong support for Tanishq from the manufacturing unit, which had discovered a passion for making fine jewellery, the sales and marketing team of the jewellery business, directors representing the Tamil Nadu government and some senior Tata directors such as Jamshed Bhabha.

Desai again consulted his senior management team, which included Jacob Kurian, Vasant Nangia and Bhaskar Bhat. He then decided that he would take the pressure head-on—the consumer opportunity in jewellery was as large as ever, despite the initial lack of success and the current financial stress. The need of the hour was a sound consumer proposition and good execution, and then it was just a question of giving the venture the time to succeed.

Desai says his knowledge of the pioneering history of the Tata Group gave him the confidence to shut out the noise and march ahead.

Enter the Karatmeter

Tanishq now made two big changes to its consumer offering. In 1999, bowing to the voice of the Indian woman, it abandoned its primary focus on 18 carat studded jewellery, and introduced a wide range of 22 carat gold jewellery. Many of these were designs inspired by an Indian look. This was built on a limited pilot offering of 22 carat jewellery that had already been launched. With this change in offering, many more Indian women opened their minds and wallets to Tanishq.

It also pioneered what will be remembered forever as one of the greatest innovations in the Indian jewellery market, the karatmeter.

This machine used the science of spectroscopy to measure the purity or caratage of gold in three minutes. It did this using rays of specified frequency without destroying the piece of jewellery. Karatmeters were placed in Tanishq showrooms where customers could see them in operation. Now, the karatmeter could instantly certify the purity of the jewellery at the point of sale.

'This was a masterstroke by the team,' says Desai. 'An obscure scientific laboratory instrument suddenly became the touchstone of our age.'

Tanishq then launched an aggressive marketing campaign highlighting that a lot of the jewellery sold in India actually offered less caratage of gold than promised, enabling jewellers to cheat the consumer and make a quick buck in the bargain. The advertisements highlighted the impeccable quality and caratage of Tanishq, invoking the Tata tradition of trust and the modern quality controls it used. The advertisements also invited consumers to walk into Tanishq showrooms and check the purity of their gold jewellery on the karatmeter at no cost.

Within days, thousands of women had walked into Tanishq showrooms to check their jewellery, and over 60 per cent of them had found that their gold was well below the stated caratage. In other words, they had been cheated by their jewellers, whom they had trusted all along.

As news of this spread like wildfire, women formed queues in front of Tanishq showrooms to check the purity of their gold. In many showrooms, including the early flagship store at Dickenson Road in Bangalore, many women broke down and wept inconsolably when they checked their gold on the karatmeter and saw that it was impure. This meant that their savings of a lifetime, much of which was in gold, diminished in value.

Tears gave way to rage and we all know hell hath no fury like a woman scorned (or cheated by her jeweller).

Such fury at family jewellers who cheat also translated into trust in Tanishq, which offered a written guarantee of 22 carat gold, backed by the Tata name and stringent quality controls.

C.K. Venkataraman, the current chief operating officer of the jewellery business, says that Tanishq has built on this promise of trust by not only offering the highest standards of purity in gold and diamonds, but also by being transparent with customers. 'Purity is concretely supported by the karatmeter, but you will find transparency in every bit of Tanishq,' he says, 'product, pricing, exchange policies, advertising—we take pride in being very clear and very customer-friendly.'

Trust continues to remain the foremost consumer proposition of Tanishq.

Belief, Focus and Innovation

The introduction of 22 carat gold jewellery corrected an initial error of judgement, and the karatmeter had proved a game changer. But Tanishq was still seen by many women as too Western, too pricey and therefore 'not for me'. These remaining barriers had to be broken if the brand had to perform to potential.

In the year 2000, there was an unfortunate exodus of senior management from the stables of Tanishq. Vasant Nangia, the man who had introduced the karatmeter, and several members of his team, left to form their own jewellery-retailing venture. Tanishq was still losing money. Into this vacuum stepped a new team headed by Jacob Kurian, who had worked with the Tata Group for over fifteen years.

The need of the hour was to infuse belief in the business and make it profitable. This would also mean convincing several lakh women that Tanishq was the best jewellery they could buy.

I had the good fortune of working as a senior member of Jacob's team in Tanishq during this phase of the business, before I eventually took charge from him as head of the business. Jacob was a charismatic leader who could never stand fools, and he relentlessly drove several waves of growth. He gathered a bunch of fine people around him and led them with rare energy, empathy and intellect. In those hectic days, we were a small team determined to make a big success of this business, and we were also aware that the sword of Damocles still hung somewhere from the ceiling.

Jacob infused belief in the future of Tanishq. One particular team event called 'I Believe' served to rally the troops by dramatically showcasing several reasons why Tanishq would succeed magnificently. It ended with all those present lighting candles in a dark conference hall, to reiterate their faith and confidence in the success of Tanishq.

From that period, three specific initiatives in the areas of marketing, financing and product innovation deserve mention here.

The first was a gold jewellery exchange scheme called '19 = 22'. Women could bring in their gold jewellery and get it tested on the karatmeter. If the purity of their jewellery was lower than 22 carat and higher than 19 carat, they could exchange it for Tanishq's pure 22 carat jewellery of their choice, by paying only the manufacturing charges. The scheme again built on the karatmeter idea, and was a wild success. It resulted in several thousand women turning to Tanishq and away from their existing jewellers.

The second was the introduction of a new funding mechanism, by which gold for making jewellery could be procured on lease from international banks. Therefore, the need to invest hard cash in buying gold disappeared instantly, and Tanishq's working capital requirements came down significantly. This threw open the vistas for rapid growth, and was the second great innovation for Tanishq after the karatmeter.

The third was the creation and marketing of lightweight gold jewellery, which maximized the surface area of the piece but minimized the weight of gold used. This appealed greatly to budget-conscious women and also conveyed the key message that Tanishq was affordable.

Riding on the back of these initiatives, Tanishq crossed business revenues of Rs 500 crore by the year 2005. This was tremendous progress, as it marked a twenty-fold increase from the revenues of Rs 24 crore achieved in 1998. Most importantly, under Kurian's leadership, the business turned profitable. The Tata Group's senior management's conviction—lacking so far—went up significantly.

Hussain says his own view of the jewellery business was transformed by these developments. 'Tanishq was appealing to the mainstream now; the model now was quite different from the elitist 18 carat jewellery premise with which the business began. Execution was excellent, the karatmeter had made its point, and "gold on lease" was a game changer.'

An article titled 'Glittering Again', published on the Tata website in October 2003, now praised Tanishq as a trailblazer: 'Pioneering can be a poisoned chalice. Tanishq, as much a trailblazer in the jewellery industry as its parent Titan was in the watch industry, knows this better than most.'

The New Face of Tanishq

An even more spectacular phase of growth began in the years thereafter. In 2002, Bhaskar Bhat had become the managing director of Titan Industries, and had defined economic success and consumer affection as the twin objectives of the company. In 2005, C.K. Venkataraman (Venkat) replaced me as the head of the jewellery business.

Venkat describes a magical moment of transformation:

> After a fundamental piece of consumer research, we understood that the evolving Indian woman has a new sense of self. She plays by the rules, but modifies them in a way which suits her. She seeks a harmonious coexistence between tradition and modernity. We seized on this insight to position Tanishq as a progressive Indian brand that combined tradition and heritage, a brand that offers new tales of tradition.

The brand had found its new face. The insight led to a coherent product strategy and several appealing advertising campaigns, which ushered over half a million women into Tanishq showrooms. If the karatmeter had rescued the brand from failure, this new brand promise was a tipping point towards stupendous success.

Tanishq's first 'new tale of tradition' was a television film whose backdrop closely resembled the settings of a popular and award-winning Hindi film called *Parineeta*. In the film, a beautiful and very traditional Indian bride, bedecked in her fabulous Tanishq jewellery, goes out for a formal drive with her groom. When they are just out of sight of the family home, she quickly exchanges places with him, and gets into the driver's seat of the car with equal ease. The film appealed immediately to all Indian women who respect tradition, yet desire freedom and modernity.

Tanishq also emphasized its Indian heritage by designing jewellery for period Bollywood films such as *Paheli* and *Jodhaa Akbar*. In *Jodhaa Akbar*, a love story involving the famous Mughal emperor Akbar and the Rajput princess Jodhaa, Tanishq created not merely the jewellery for the royal couple, but also the jewelled armour and magnificent swords. It was a fabulous display of the craft of traditional jewellery. The brand simultaneously highlighted its modern appeal by creating distinctive crowns for winners of the glamorous Miss India contest.

Venkat also mentions Tanishq's assiduous efforts to woo the large Indian middle class, with schemes such as the Golden Harvest programme, where consumers could buy jewellery through advance instalments, with an attractive free instalment thrown in by the company. Several focused efforts went into targeting the wedding jewellery market, as well as the high-value jewellery segment.

Tanishq retail showrooms across India, managed for the most part by competent franchisees, offered consumers one of the best shopping experiences in the country. Rigorous retail workshops were conducted with these franchisees each year to ensure that each element of the brand's plans were fully in place. Venkat says the idea of these workshops was a seminal moment in the story of the brand, particularly since retail is all about detail.

Tanishq developed a new focus on transforming its customers into passionate fans of the brand. Thousands of women customers and their spouses were also invited to visit the jewellery factory at Hosur. Here, for the first time in their lives, they saw for themselves the process of jewellery making, and also held in their hands a ten-kilogram ingot of pure Tanishq gold!

The brand also launched marketing campaigns to educate consumers about diamonds. In 2011, the legendary Bollywood actor Amitabh Bachchan paired up with his wife, Jaya Bachchan, in a memorable advertisement to showcase the virtues of diamonds marketed by Tanishq. Women responded by streaming into Tanishq stores, and sales of diamond jewellery shot up beyond expectations.

This was a dream run. Tanishq crossed annual revenues of Rs 5000 crore with ease and hurtled towards its next big milestone. It also notched up rapid growth in profits. In his presentation at the Tata Group's Annual General Managers' Meeting (AGMM) in 2012, Ratan Tata highlighted the relative financial performance of various businesses in the group. All major Tata businesses were grouped into four performance quadrants, for ease of understanding. The jewellery business, which had virtually been written off a decade earlier, now featured in the topmost quadrant of profitability.

Transforming the Jewellery Industry

Behind the glamour of the Indian jewellery industry lie hidden some of the most primitive working conditions for the artisans who make jewellery. They come from traditional jewellery-making areas and families, and their valuable skills are often passed on from one generation to the next. Yet, they have mostly worked in appallingly cramped conditions, exposed to heat, sweat, dust and hazardous chemicals. Because they are unorganized, they are exploited by crafty middlemen, who tend to pocket much of the profits, giving the artisans little in return. Readers of Charles Dickens's novels will find a lot of similarity between his descriptions of the poorest parts of London and the insides of these poorly lit jewellery workshops.

Tanishq, after achieving excellent growth and business success, has now set about transforming these industry conditions. It has established 'karigar parks' that bring these artisans together and provide them with comfortable working conditions. Venkat says:

> We have an ambitious programme called Mr Perfect, which modernizes these facilities and injects respectability, prestige and glamour into the manufacturing of jewellery. From dingy workshops, we have created well-ventilated, clean environments that are comparable with modern offices. This will encourage artisans to happily remain in this profession for generations to come. We hope many more enlightened jewellers will follow in our wake.
>
> Jewellery always brings beautiful smiles to the faces of women. We want to bring equally broad smiles to the faces of the artisans who create these wonderful pieces with their own hands.

Bhaskar Bhat, the managing director of Titan Industries, speaks about the next phase of transformation that Tanishq should drive. The jewellery industry is often seen in poor light, he says, because of the perception that unaccounted or 'black' money is involved in large purchases. The government has recently initiated some action on this front, and Tanishq will once again be at the forefront of setting the right example. He says, 'Our vision is not merely to be a large and very successful player in jewellery, but to be an engine of transformation—only then can we be creators of wealth in the tradition of the Tatas.'

Looking Back, Looking Ahead

In March 2012, Titan Industries hosted a gala dinner in the Taj Vivanta Hotel at Bangalore to celebrate twenty-five years of the company's existence. The board of directors, current and past members of senior management had turned up in strength. The dress code for the evening specified a touch of silver, but a number of elegant lady invitees chose to wear Tanishq gold and diamond jewellery instead.

Xerxes Desai, whose vision and courage had created Tanishq, was present. So was Ishaat Hussain, his friend from Tata headquarters, with whom he had debated the future of this business many years ago.

When Ishaat Hussain stood up to speak, he was gracious and aristocratic, as always. He said, 'On the jewellery business, I must admit that I was wrong. Xerxes's conviction has turned out to be quite right, and we must applaud him for having created such a magnificent enterprise.'

These are generous words, and they will do much to encourage future pioneers within the Tatas.

But Desai is not yet happy with Tanishq. He feels that while the brand may be a big commercial success, it will become iconic only if it sharpens its appeal and regains the high ground on design.

'Tanishq must segment the jewellery market based on designs and price points. It must go back to the design concept as a differentiator. A work of art is known by its concept, and jewellery is such an expansive art form. Look at what Fabergé did with a blooming egg!'

———————

Extracted from *Tata Log* by Harish Bhat

Chapter 9

S. Ramadorai

The success of America's Silicon Valley can be attributed to several factors but one that is irrefutable is a supportive ecosystem that encourages creativity, innovation and entrepreneurship.

In contrast, in the India of the 1970s when TCS[1] had just started up, an ecosystem was non-existent, and as a matter of fact the regulatory environment was not even pro-business.

When TCS went public in 2004, we were into our thirty-sixth year of existence. Often people would ask me where TCS had been all this while, and I would tell them that our first twenty years were spent building the foundations of the IT industry, clearing the hurdles with the government, and catalysing the regulatory framework which till then had never catered to importing computers or exporting software. We consciously made investments of time, money and expertise in academic partnerships with a view to building a talent base in the nation, and we did this quietly and without fanfare. Too quietly perhaps did we wear the mantle of a pioneer, something for which we paid a price in later years. Let us not forget that for all other companies that followed, TCS's initial investment created a springboard to take off from.

Four decades ago, there were many challenges for a private sector company in dealing with the Indian government. Indira Gandhi was the prime minister and was determined to carry on the Nehruvian socialist model. Jawaharlal Nehru's education at Trinity College, Cambridge, had been influenced by the Fabian socialist movement and he had come to believe that in a poor and populous country like India, the public sector should occupy the commanding heights of industry.

Indira Gandhi fervently followed the same path, creating a centrally controlled economy based on the Soviet model. Under her rule the banking and insurance sectors were nationalized and India adopted a policy of five-year national plans. Everything that the private sector did required permission from the government in the form of a licence. The list of licences was almost endless: private sector companies needed industrial licences, capital goods licences and import licences to name just a few; this eventually led to this period being known as the 'licence raj'.

The government strategy was driven in part by the lack of foreign reserves in our coffers. Precious foreign exchange had to be used to create food reserves, fund oil imports and pay for defence equipment etc. It was to be used sparingly for other purposes.

This had a direct impact on TCS because we wanted to bring mainframe computers and state-of-the-art technology into the country and use it to train our people, just like we had been trained in the US. Obviously, we needed foreign exchange to pay for these purchases.

The second factor working against us was a view that computers were labour-saving devices. As a result there was an inherent resistance to computerization, particularly in bigger public sector corporations and the government sector which had very strong, entrenched unions which felt that automation would take away jobs. There was also a widespread feeling that the government looked at profit-making with suspicion. Clearly we were on a path that was tangential to the Indian government.

The Indian private sector and foreign companies that were present in the Indian market felt a great sense of constraint. At the time the government had the power, through licences, to dictate to businesses when and where they could increase capacity and what products they could make. No company could expand annual revenues beyond Rs 20 crore without specific clearance under the Monopolies and Restrictive Trade Practices (MRTP) Act.

In fact, many large industrial groups felt that the government's restrictive policies prevented them from serving the country and enriching its economy to the full extent of their capacity and will. An exchange between P.N. Haksar and J.R.D. Tata provides a good insight of the frustration felt at that time by industrialists.

Haksar was a brilliant lawyer who after two decades of outstanding diplomatic service was recalled to serve as secretary, and later as principal secretary to Prime Minister Indira Gandhi. He was a big influence on the shaping of India's domestic and foreign policies.

On JRD's eightieth birthday, Haksar wrote him a congratulatory note and urged him to reflect constructively and creatively on the state of the country. JRD, who probably saw this comment as salt on his wounds, could not resist responding with an unabashed forthrightness.

He wrote:

In the 100 years prior to Independence, opportunities created by the Industrial Revolution were denied to Indian merchants, financiers and affluent members of the bourgeoisie. The advent of Independence brought about a dramatic change in the situation which would normally have provided the same vital base as in other countries for great projects, ventures and adventures by Indians.

An essential pre-requisite however would have been a freedom of choice, of investment and of action which it took no time at all for our politicians and our burgeoning bureaucracy to block or stifle in the process of concentrating of all economic power in the government.

Instead of releasing energies and enterprise, the system of licences and all pervasive controls imposed on the private sector in the country combined with confiscatory personal taxation, not only discouraged and penalized honest free enterprise, but encouraged and brought success and wealth to a new breed of bribers, tax evaders and black marketers.

In a single generation, great fortunes largely transferred abroad were built at a time when personal incomes of Rs 1 lakh per year were taxed at 98 per cent. The nationalization, on expropriatory terms, of insurance and banks, conveniently created a virtual monopoly of investible and lendable funds while fiscal policies combined with the use made of the Companies Act, the Industries Development & Regulations Act, the Monopolies and Restrictive Trade

Practices Act and innumerable other enactments, regulations and administrative decisions, effectively concentrated all real economic power in the hands of politicians in power and bureaucracy. Under such conditions efforts at promoting and bringing to fruition large projects however desirable became a nightmarish and time-consuming one or ended in outright rejection.

JRD's words were to echo strongly later with TCS. We too felt extremely constrained. While we saw how the West was leveraging mainframe computers and information technology to achieve efficiency through bulk data processing in sectors such as defence and banking, India was missing out on the IT revolution.

But we were persistent. In just the same way that the Tatas had been pioneers in steel, energy and engines, we believed that TCS could be a pioneer in IT. We had confidence that if we could bring these new technologies into India, they could change the course of the nation and some day be a very important parameter for growth.

To serve an overseas market, we needed the latest learning, the latest generation of computers to be imported and we needed to explore top-of-the-line partnerships. So the first task was to find a way to import the equipment into India. This meant crossing swords with the government and the mighty 'licence raj'.

At that time every industry had an administrative ministry in the central government. We came under the department of electronics (DoE) which was headed by Professor M.G.K. Menon. Prof. Menon was also the chairman of the electronics commission, the secretary of the department of electronics, and the scientific adviser to the government on defence.

As a scientific department, the DoE reported directly to the prime minister, and unfortunately the department was very wary of our intentions. In addition, since TCS was a division of Tata Sons, and the Tata Group was listed under MRTP as a dominant company because of its size and market share, any expansion which resulted in a capacity increase of 25 per cent or more required approval from the Monopolies and Restrictive Trade Practices Commission (MRTPC). In practice this meant another round of bureaucratic torture.

The process for importing a computer was mind-bogglingly complex and every stage had its own challenges, mostly because this was all being done for the very first time in India and the existing laws were open to interpretation by government officials who were unfamiliar with computers.

The process went something like this:

1. First we had to submit an application for an import licence to the DoE. This included an application for import of capital goods as well. As part of this process we had to justify what we wanted to do with the computer. Towards this we would produce a letter of intent from Burroughs placing an order for software services from TCS. Also included was the pro forma invoice with model numbers of the machines; sometimes technical literature was also sent.

2. Eleven copies were required as copies would be sent to various ministries including finance, commerce and industries. The DoE would then obtain the capital goods permission.

3. Next we had to obtain approval from the MRTPC as we belonged to a 'large' business house.

4. Then we had to navigate the complicated import tariffs and estimate the customs duty, which as it turned out was more than the cost of the machine itself.

5. We also had to get approval for free foreign exchange (to pay in US dollars for the import) from the government.

6. We had to justify the import by undertaking an export obligation to export twice the import cost (CIF) over a five-year period after the import. Failure to do so would involve confiscation of the machine in addition to severe financial penalties.

7. We also had to obtain an export licence from the US department of commerce and provide an 'end-user certificate'. This was a problem when we had an order for a defence laboratory. Even so, the exporting nation had the right to monitor the use of the machine and confiscate it and begin criminal proceedings against us should there be any misuse.

8. Once we had secured all the above licences and approvals we weighed several tons; for large systems we had to charter a B707 freighter!

9. When the equipment arrived in India we had to clear it through the stringent customs procedures.

10. Finally we had to transport the bulky yet delicate equipment to the data centre and install it. This posed other problems as roads could be bumpy, underpasses not high enough to allow trucks with tall tape drives to pass under without getting jammed, lifts not large enough, false floor tiles not strong enough to take the load without buckling, etc.

Once we decided to import our first mainframe, we quickly found ourselves caught in the maze of government departments and their regulations. It is no exaggeration to say that TCS was faced with a totally unprecedented situation.

In the early 1970s Burroughs, then the second-largest computer manufacturer after IBM, saw India as a potential market and was willing to share its technology. In 1973 TCS signed an agreement with Burroughs. We agreed to distribute and sell Burroughs computers in India and they agreed to sell us a new Burroughs B1728 'small-system' computer.

Though advanced for its day, the B1728 would not be categorized as a mainframe today because it had only 128 Kb of memory and 8 Mb of disk space to start with. The memory sticks in our pockets today have larger storage capacities.

Our strategy was to import the machine, train ourselves to program and write software applications for it, and then to sell these services to markets outside India in order to earn foreign exchange. But we had not anticipated just how difficult it would be to import a new mainframe into India.

At that time, nobody in the private sector had imported a brand new mainframe. There were about 300 mainframe computers in the country that had been imported by university research departments, government agencies or the Ministry of Defence, but none of them had to pay import duty. Similarly there was also no precedent for customs duty computation for import of new systems in the private sector, because till then no one in the private sector had imported a brand new computer. The practice till then was that IBM (International Business Machines Corporation) and ICL (International Computers Ltd) used subsystems and parts, which they refurbished in their factories in India before making them available to Indian customers. These imports were treated as 'project' imports which had a different duty computation. So when TCS imported a new mainframe it was a whole new matter.

The Indian government said it would give us permission to import a new mainframe, but only if we exported twice its value over a five-year period. It was a bold step for TCS to make this commitment at that stage because we hardly had any export revenue to speak of.

That is how the Indian software industry was born, not by any grand design but by an accident of history because India was short of foreign exchange and we had to earn foreign exchange to pay for the importation of a new Burroughs mainframe.

The government's foreign exchange was reserved exclusively for defence and other government projects. Others seeking foreign exchange were referred to two institutional banks, IDBI and ICICI. Both institutional banks had access to foreign exchange through the World Bank and could provide this to Indian companies in the form of loans. But our owners, the Tatas, did not want to go down this route because the loans came with a convertibility clause that meant if the borrower defaulted, the bank would have an option to convert their money into equity. Tata Sons was a privately held limited company with charitable trusts as the owners, and the trusts did not want any outsiders to have a stake in the company.

So instead of tapping the institutional banks when we wanted to purchase the Burroughs mainframe in 1973, we approached Citibank. The US bank agreed to provide us with a loan in New York at 1 per cent over the London Interbank Rate (Libor) so the interest rate was about 3 or 4 per cent compared to the 8 or 9 per cent we would have had to pay in India.

We planned to service the loan through Tata Inc. in New York using the foreign exchange we earned in the US. Tata

Inc. was a company originally set up to procure spare parts for Air India, but later it became an arm of Tata Steel. The arrangement with the Tatas was that when any Tata Group company purchased material from the US, it was routed through Tata Inc. which in turn received a commission for handling the paperwork.

It was a perfectly good idea, but the Indian government rejected it because the bureaucrats said, 'We do not allow Indian companies to borrow abroad.' We enlisted the support of the Secretary of Economic Affairs because he was the contemporary of the father of a TCS colleague when they had been at the Reserve Bank. The Secretary agreed it was a good idea, but the department director had serious reservations. Ultimately I think the bureaucrats were suspicious of any new ideas and it was perhaps easier to say 'no'. Whatever the case, at that time the bureaucrats had the power to block initiatives, and they chose to do just that.

As a result, we had to borrow in rupees, which was more expensive, and then convert the loan into foreign exchange. We obtained the loan from Citibank in Bombay, issued a letter of credit to Tata Inc. in New York who purchased the machine and then exported it to us. But we incurred extra costs all the way. We also had to enter into a forward contract to protect ourselves against a devaluation of the rupee during the five-year term of the bank loan. It was the most inefficient way of doing things, but the government insisted we do it that way if we wanted the import licence.

It fell to Jayant[2] to make all these applications. He had to learn things which nobody knew. The most complicated problem he faced was that nobody knew what the import duty on a new computer should be. Under India's import customs tariff nomenclature there was no mention of 'computers'. Oddly enough it did not come under 'machines' either, even though a computer was formally called an electronic data-processing (EDP) machine.

Instead computers came under Section 76 which was for 'electronic appliances and apparatus not specified elsewhere'. That meant a gigantic mainframe computer that required a room to house it and air conditioning to keep it from overheating was lumped together with mixer-grinders, toasters and electric razors. Since it was classified as an apparatus, it also attracted a higher rate of duty. An apparatus was considered to be a non-essential luxury item and attracted a 60 per cent import tax rather than the 40 per cent that applied to machines which were meant to be used for industrial purposes.

Ironically there was a different nomenclature in place for excise duty. Excise duty was charged by the central government on the value of equipment manufactured in India, before sales tax. When something was imported, in order to protect the domestic industry, the government added the equivalent of excise duty which was called countervailing duty (CVD) to the import tax. To figure out the correct CVD rate we had to refer to the excise manual which followed the Brussels nomenclature and classified computers as machines. So a computer was a machine for CVD purposes and an apparatus for the purposes of import duty.

Over and above this, there were cascading duties as well: if the import duty was less than 40 per cent, the importer paid auxiliary duty at a 2 per cent rate; over 40 per cent the auxiliary duty was 5 per cent. Then you had to add the CVD of 15 per cent. We added all the numbers up and thought the total duty would be about 75 per cent.

But when we went to the customs and excise department at the airport to verify the calculations we were told that the CVD was applied on the ad valorem amount after the import duty and auxiliary duty were calculated, which meant the total duty payable on an imported mainframe computer was 101.25 per cent—although this was not actually written down anywhere.

This new and shocking development had to be communicated to Kohli[3] so Jayant drove to a public phone booth outside the airport and called him. Jayant got through to Kohli's assistant and gave him the news but the assistant said, 'You had better tell him yourself in person.' No one wanted to be the harbinger of bad news. The drive from Santa Cruz up north to the Air India building in south Mumbai was the longest ever for Jayant who was chosen to deliver this bit of news. So what would have been a hot drive in a non-air-conditioned car became an even hotter one. In his inimitable style though, Jayant stood through Kohli's dressing-down on why the calculations were so off-track.

The system itself cost $340,000 but we ended up paying more than twice that, and losing out on the exchange rate too.

Burroughs also needed a licence to export equipment from the US because the mainframe was considered a strategic item and it needed approval from the US defence department. So we had to provide a statement about what we would do with the computer.

The whole process took between nine months and a year. We started in 1973 and we finally imported the computer in 1974. Later on, it sometimes took two years because the process became even more complicated when the government decided that we were a Monopoly Restricted Trade Practice and our licence applications had to be approved by multiple committees.

The complicated processes, which often defied reason, forced us to become very creative in finding ways to work around the challenges. For example, we found out that we could import the equipment under a special customs bond that enabled us to move it from the airport and open it for inspection by customs at our own offices rather than at the airport warehouse where equipment damage was more likely.

We managed to persuade the customs authorities to agree to a bond which involved the customs officers at the airport wrapping each of the equipment boxes with wire and putting a lead seal on them. Then the boxes were loaded onto two or three trucks which came in a convoy escorted by customs officers to our offices in the Air India building in Bombay.

When we got to our office at the Air India building and offloaded the trucks the customs officials decided they were tired so we took them to the Taj for dinner, served copious quantities of beer and gave them taxi fare to get home. They said they would return early the next morning to clear the equipment.

Next day, we arrived at the office very early to make sure the documentation was in order. To our horror we discovered that the electrician, in his eagerness to help, had removed the seals, 'so the boxes could be opened easily'!

I was with Jayant and a couple of field engineers and we asked ourselves what we should do now. We found all the seals and the wires which were in a dustbin, wrapped all the boxes up again with the wire and threaded the seals on to the end and bent the wire so it looked as though it had not been tampered with. We didn't know what would happen but we were concerned that the customs officials might say we had broken the bond and would therefore confiscate the equipment. We had visions of ourselves languishing in jail.

The customs people turned up soon. As soon as they arrived we said, 'See, here are the seals,' and quickly broke the seals in front of them before they could inspect them too closely. Luckily the strategy worked beautifully.

Our agony was not over. We still had the task of verifying the list of items on the import licence with the invoice—nothing tallied because we had all the model numbers from the marketing literature, the engineering guys had their own part numbers and the finance department which made the invoice had yet another set of numbers.

For example, the import licence was for a B1728 computer but the invoice said 'B Series' and somewhere else it said 'CPU 1728' and also '1700 range'. The customs officers asked us, 'But where does it say B1728?' Suddenly one of us saw there was a table on the underside of the box, scrambled under and quickly scribbled 'B1728' in one of the columns. We then called the officers over and showed them the legend. They said, 'Okay.' Really, all they wanted to do was to tick off something that said 'B1728'.

Next time around, in 1976, when we imported a much bigger Burroughs 6748 machine that cost over $1 million, we told the Burroughs guys to make sure the invoice looked just like the sales material and matched the numbers on the equipment.

Each cabinet in that machine weighed over a ton and the dimensions were larger than the inside of the elevator in the Air India building. So we actually considered hoisting the cabinets up, slung from a hook on the underside of the elevator. In the end, however, we removed the internal elevator car railings and then somehow managed to slide the cabinets diagonally into the elevator car.

At our offices in the Air India building we had to create a data centre which involved creating a raised floor so cabling could run underneath. Traditionally the void below would be created like a grid, with slotted angles much like those found in a child's Meccano set. This grid would then be covered with tiles to create the raised floor.

In the case of the B6700, the mainframe also required a cold chamber under it and fans under the computer cabinets which would suck the cold air in to cool the machines. Kohli decided to try out an innovation and suggested that we use 9x9x9 inch bricks made of coal ash, a by-product of electricity generation at Tata Electric, as fillers.

Columns of these would form the grid, and tiles would be placed above. However the column distances necessitated larger tiles, so they had to be specially ordered and, when we moved the cabinets across the room to position them, the larger tiles sagged much more than the smaller ones, causing them to crack. So the attempted innovation turned out to be more of an irritant. Even so, the attempt to recycle waste material was a cause worth trying out and I am sure it would have met the appreciation of 'green' advocators.

Our frustration was far from over. The day after we installed the new mainframe in the Air India building, the government's annual finance budget was announced and the duty on computers was reduced from the 101.25 per cent we had paid to a total of 60 per cent.

In those days it was hard to predict what the policy changes would be in forthcoming budgets and Kohli had been expediting the import because of concerns about the possible devaluation of the rupee. But at least we stood to benefit in the future.

We had fought with the government for a rationalization of duties and appealed to the tax administrators on the basis that the mainframe had been wrongly classified. But at every stage we lost because the administrators said a complex electronic circuit board could not be defined as a machine because it had no moving parts. So eventually we decided to take the issue to the civil courts.

Finally, in 1980, four years after we launched the first appeal, I went with Jayant to the Bombay High Court and our case was heard. After listening to arguments from both sides the judge ruled that the government had no case and that the computers we had imported had been wrongly classified as 'appliance and apparatus' rather than EDP machines. He ordered a full refund of customs and excise duties, so we got a refund of Rs 65 lakh in 1980. For all our efforts Jayant and I treated ourselves to lunch.

It was an important ruling not just because of the refund, but because it forced the government to create a specific classification for computers. Not only did we help create a policy to import computers, but we helped create the software export industry and we got computers correctly classified for customs duties too.

Extracted from *The TCS Story . . . and Beyond* by S. Ramadorai

Chapter 10

F.C. Kohli

The 1960s were a turbulent time for India: food shortages, trade deficits and socialist government controls on the economy coupled with two wars, one with China in 1962 and the other with Pakistan in 1965, sapped national resources.

The economy grew at an average rate of about 3.1 per cent a year in constant prices, or at an annual rate of 1 per cent per capita. Governance became synonymous with the 'licence raj' with its elaborate system of licences, regulations and red tape.

It was in this restrictive environment that J.R.D. Tata, chairman of the Tata Group whose interests spanned from steel and automobiles to power and chemicals, took a fateful decision. Like his forefathers who pioneered basic infrastructure in the country, JRD too had a keen business sense. So when his brother-in-law, aide and confidant Colonel Sawhney suggested pooling together the group's needs for data processing in a single business unit, he readily agreed.

In terms of technology, India was a backwater at the time and computers in particular were looked on with some suspicion because of their potential to replace labour. But as companies in the West began to invest in commercial mainframes to streamline operations like inventory control and payroll, J.R.D. Tata decided to go ahead with the project and set up an in-house data processing unit.

At this time TISCO, now Tata Steel, had the largest data processing requirement followed by Tata Engineering and Locomotives Company (TELCO, now Tata Motors). The new team that was assembled comprised mostly people from Tata Administrative Service (TAS) who were to be trained. Yash Sahni, who had a statistical background and was with National Council of Applied Economic Research (NCAER) at that time, was brought in as the team supervisor in 1962.

Recounting those days, Sahni remembers that talks were held with IBM to acquire their 'Unit Record Machines'; the acquisition would be on a lease basis as at that time IBM never sold their computers, but only provided them on lease.

Sahni and his team moved from the Tata headquarters in Bombay House to the Army Navy building and then finally to a place specially created for them in Ballard Estate, a business district in south Bombay. The team still did not have a name and was referred to as a division of Tata Sons with a mandate to set up a data processing unit to service all Tata Group companies. The total investment by Tata Sons was about Rs 50 lakh ($110,000).

But there was a problem. Most individual Tata companies did not want to hand over their data processing work to this new unit, preferring instead to keep the work (and the expertise) in-house. At best they were willing to allow the new unit to do their shareholder accounting work, which was actually quite cumbersome for them and involved obtaining legal clearances.

The only exception was Tata Electric which, perhaps because it was staffed mostly by engineers, gave the fledgling data processing unit more sophisticated work. Unfortunately Colonel Sawhney, who had come up with the idea, died soon after, so the team was left without anyone inside Tata Sons to champion its cause.

In order to meet its rising costs, the unit desperately sought work from outside the Tata Group, but realized that it would need access to a mainframe computer if it were to succeed. One well-respected British company wanted to charge a consultancy fee of £10,000 merely to advise what machine to purchase. Not surprisingly, the proposal was turned down.

In any case, in 1964 there was not much choice. It was either IBM or ICL, a leading British computer company which was second to IBM in the Indian market. But ICL was considered old technology, and several Tata Sons companies including Tata Motors and Tata Steel already had IBM machines so the general inclination was towards IBM. Ultimately, however, the team started buying time from an IBM data centre on their IBM 1401 computer. As hardware was scarce this was then a very lucrative business for IBM.

At the same time, there was a move to recruit more qualified and knowledgeable people to the team. People like Ashok Malhotra and Nitin Patel, both from MIT, joined the team. This was later augmented with people like Lalit Kanodia, Pravin Gandhi and of course Yash Sahni who had a strong quantitative methods background and were young, innovative and aggressive to boot. Collectively they brought together expertise in areas such as engineering, computer science and operations research. Such a high-powered group from top universities would have been rare to find in any company at that time. One of the early customers was Tata Institute of Social Sciences (TISS) which was planning a major study and needed advice on sampling, design of questionnaires, data collection and analysis.

There was still no work from private industries, but the unit managed to make enough money to pay its own bills right from the beginning. The team, however, had a dispersed structure and many of the staff were still on the payrolls of different Tata companies.

In 1966, the whole unit was brought under Tata Services and moved to the Nirmal building at Nariman Point—then a developing area reclaimed from the sea in south Bombay which was later to become one of the most expensive business districts in the world. The prestigious Nirmal building was the first skyscraper in India and the embryonic TCS unit was its first tenant. By now the unit had earned a good reputation amongst customers for whom it did share accounting and registry work on the data processing machines; as a result TCS was able to win customers away from IBM which provided similar services in their own data centres.

By 1968 TCS had two IBM 1401s on lease and one ICL 1903 which was purchased. All these were housed on the eighth floor of Nirmal building and nicknamed Able-Baker-Charlie. This space was christened the Tata Computer Centre. The management and consultancy staff were housed on the ninth floor of the same building. For its time the ambience was modern and the envy of many other offices. At the time the company had a small capital so both floors were rented; later these were acquired and became the first home of TCS.

The management's faith in the fledgling company was demonstrated in the acquisition two years later of two floors in the neighbouring Air India building which for many years was the most sought-after business address in India. These two floors added another 20,000 sq. ft of office capacity, at that time raising many doubts and eyebrows among the finance moguls at Bombay House, the Tata headquarters.

The creation of the Tata Computer Centre ushered in a period of aggressive selling and business began to look up. Beginning in 1968 the unit undertook a lot of banking work, mostly reconciling inter-branch accounts, payroll accounting and head office accounting. The volume of banking work was so large that by the mid-1970s there were 500 professionals in Delhi and other places where the Tata Computer Centre had IBM/ICL machines.

Up until this point Tata Sons had very small holdings in Tata Group companies, and their earnings were mainly dependent on dividends paid by these companies. To enhance income, the Tatas decided in 1968 to restructure some of the units as operating divisions.

Four separate divisions were born at one go: Tata Consulting Engineers, Tata Economic Consultancy Services, Tata Financial Services and Tata Consultancy Services. The Tata Computer Centre became a part of TCS and P.M. Agarwala, the managing director of Tata Electric Companies, took over as director-in-charge of TCS in addition to his other responsibilities. PMA, as he was often referred to, was one of India's earliest telecom/electronics engineers from Roorkee University (now IIT Roorkee) and was a technical member of the Government of India's Posts and Telegraph and Telephone Board before joining Tata Electric.

The young, highly talented team of TCS was often more like a rowdy, boisterous bunch from the Wild West. Every new order created euphoria and each invoice was celebrated with a beer party on the terrace of Nirmal building. Winning a contract warranted a movie in the afternoon at one of the nearby theatres. Spirits were running high but the same could not be said about the cash flow. Agarwala quickly seized the situation and realized that he needed a strong hand at the top—a 'headmaster' figure—to bring in order.

He chose Faqir Chand Kohli, a brilliant technocrat who was the deputy general manager at Tata Electric. His role as Chief Load Despatch meant that he controlled the power grid for the city of Bombay. Agarwala perhaps felt that if Kohli controlled the power to the entire city surely he could control the unruly lot at Nirmal building. Kohli was also knowledgeable about computers and that too would have been an influence on his choice. There was just one problem. Kohli did not want to leave Tata Electric and viewed a move to TCS as a diversion from his ambition to ultimately head Tata Electric which at that time was a prestigious post.

But Agarwala prevailed and despite his reservations Kohli was coerced into joining TCS as the general manager in 1969: a post that was specially created for him. The adjustment to the new environment took him six months. He would pore over technical manuals at home to acquaint himself with technology, thereby earning the respect of his juniors. This held an important lesson for me that as a leader one must have a strong working knowledge of the technical environment that one is managing.

Finally Kohli began to integrate with his new team and a new selling strategy started to emerge. Since neither the government nor private companies were interested in data processing, the TCS team decided to position the company as management consultants. This new positioning opened the doors to new business: once the client was engaged they were encouraged to take on automation and electronic data processing work as a way towards more efficient management. This was a convoluted route to data processing work but was necessary since, manual systems being prevalent, automation at that time was not very well understood. So ironically while TCS began with data processing and moved to management consulting, western management consulting companies on the other hand were diversifying into IT services.

Once he had settled into his new role at TCS, Kohli set about shaping the young company armed with the conviction that in order to use computers, India needed bright young people with good education—something India had in abundance. Kohli had a good relationship with the IITs where he used to teach often. He capitalized on this to recruit the best and the brightest young engineering graduates.

When TCS was formed in 1968 there were no separate IT departments in Indian universities and Indian electrical and electronic engineering graduates with an interest in IT typically went overseas to undertake their graduate studies in computer science. Under Kohli, TCS recruited most of the first batch of students who had completed their Master's in computer science at IIT Kanpur, one of India's premier technology institutes and also the first to introduce computer science doctoral studies—although at that stage it was still under the electrical engineering department. Other early IIT Kanpur graduates went on to set up many of India's other IT industry start-ups.

In those early days it was as though TCS was a Silicon Valley start-up. Here was a group of India's brightest people with no dictated agenda and because we were a division of Tata Sons, there was no requirement to produce a balance sheet.

Management consultancy was becoming big for TCS. It involved working with government organizations like Hindustan Aeronautics Limited (HAL), providing major production planning and control systems for light combat aircraft. These were very complex systems and spoke of the strong expertise TCS had. A major system engineering and cybernetics activity was set up with the help of George Mason University who helped with the training. The training was on the simulation systems used in the US for war games; TCS's interest was in using these very applications with changed variables, to solve societal problems. Later a centre in Hyderabad was set up for these services. One of the earliest organizations TCS worked for was the Delhi Development Authority (DDA), helping them in their corporatization with a focus on societal benefit. Similar work was done for the Government of India's Department of Atomic Energy around the time that the Nuclear Power Corporation of India was being formed as a public sector company. TCS also worked with the north-eastern states to try and figure out why government aid was not reaching down to the people.

The management consulting work established our intellectual leadership and helped position TCS as a thought leader.

In 1974, when Kohli was still the general manager, Agarwala took ill and began to operate from home. Unfortunately he did not recover and succumbed to his illness a few months later. Kohli took over as the TCS director-in-charge the same year. He reported to the TCS Consultancy Committee whose members were Tata Sons directors: A.B. Billimoria, Freddie Mehta and Nani Palkhivala, who was also chairman of the committee.

For the first time Kohli was now in a position to drive TCS's vision. From general manager to director-in-charge was a big jump. In the normal course of things, had Agarwala lived through his term, Kohli may well have returned to Tata Electric.

However, despite his initial reluctance, directing, influencing and shaping a new company in an emerging field was a compelling challenge for Kohli. Automation and computerization had growing business potential and this leadership opportunity may well have influenced Kohli's decision to stay with TCS rather than return to Tata Electric.

Armed with an electrical engineering degree from the Massachusetts Institute of Technology (MIT), Kohli had already earned a reputation as a visionary man. His early contributions at Tata Power included the use of control system methodologies to provide a stable power supply system for Bombay. At Tata Electric he introduced advanced engineering and management techniques and made significant use of digital computers for power system design and control. In 1968, ahead of all but four utilities in the US, Tata Electric installed a Westinghouse computer to control the operations of its power grid which comprised three hydro stations, thermal units and energy supplies from the Tarapore atomic energy and Koyna hydroelectric stations of the Maharashtra State Electricity Board.

What Kohli realized was that monitoring and controlling were critical to the provision of a reliable power supply. He clearly understood the power of technology.

Kohli always wanted India to be part of the computer revolution that was beginning in the West. His electrical engineering degree and MIT training coupled with his voracious appetite for books on technology gave him the confidence to try new things in India and to create value.

I often wonder what might have happened if Kohli had stayed at Tata Electric. Perhaps he would have enabled great transformations in the power sector with his zeal and enthusiasm for applying new technologies to the generation and transmission of power.

All that he gave to the IT industry would have gone instead to the power sector. Perhaps he would have built up a huge talent base that would have met the Indian government's mission of power for all by 2012. Unfortunately today, sectors such as these face a huge shortfall of good people and leaders to drive the agenda aggressively.

Working with Kohli

When I joined TCS I got to know my mentor F.C. Kohli for the first time. At that time Kohli was actively involved in recruitment and used to meet every new recruit.

Most young entry-level engineers were afraid to speak to or approach Kohli because of his reputation as a stern taskmaster. But our initial trepidation began to go away as we started to learn a little more about him and realized that he was a man who was very direct and very quick to grasp issues.

He would tell us quite bluntly what was the right thing to do, and what was not. If, however, you were sure you were right you could challenge him, and he would respect that. One of my colleagues wondered how I could deal with his formidable personality. One even described him as 'a benevolent dictator ... or perhaps not so benevolent'. Kohli was certainly not known for his patience and he was tough, but as I learned later, he also had a soft heart.

Perhaps most importantly, he taught me the importance of under-promising and over-delivering to clients. I also found that he was always willing to help you succeed if you were willing to put in the work. I remember days when I worked from 4.30 a.m. to 11.30 p.m. in order to meet a customer deadline. Times like these helped us establish a comfortable relationship based on mutual respect.

When Kohli spoke, you listened, which taught me the importance of being a good listener; but he was also a man of few words and his instructions were often quite minimal, which trained me to anticipate what was required to be delivered.

Today, it is quite common to have a full and frank discussion between a subordinate and a boss but in those days, companies were quite hierarchical and it was difficult for a relative junior to communicate with a senior without appearing to question or challenge them. Holding an open discussion with a boss was against the ethos of the time and against the upbringing I had had.

As a result, I often found myself communicating with Kohli by writing memos to ensure that I had understood what he wanted and correcting it if I had got it wrong. More importantly, it provided me with the opportunity to disagree in a non-confrontational way. As I discovered, if you believe in something there is always a way to communicate it. Being intimidated by your boss is no reason to not express yourself.

In retrospect, Kohli knew that challenging people was one way to bring out the best in them. So he threw us challenge after challenge, stretching all of us towards continuous improvement while at the same time allowing us broad latitude for experimentation. The assignments were tough and sometimes we even resented having to go through the pain, but the taste of success always made it worthwhile. It was an important lesson in leadership for me that challenging subordinates to step out of their own comfort zones was one of the best ways to develop their skills and discover what they were capable of.

Just as importantly, Kohli's 'can do' attitude was passed on to us.

In India we had no previous models really to learn from, no reference points. Everything we did was for the first time—and this gave us a bit of a cavalier attitude. We used to joke that it was like being thrown into water—even when you did not know how to swim, you just had to figure it out. Kohli was a tough taskmaster.

Extracted from *The TCS Story . . . and Beyond* by S. Ramadorai

Part III

Companies and Institutions

Chapter 11

Tata Indica

Today cars have become items of intense desire. Consequently, auto shows have begun to rival fashion shows as far as the glamour quotient is concerned. Auto Expo 1998, held in New Delhi, was extra special because Tata Motors was launching an Indian car for the first time in history. Hundreds of children happily waving the Indian flag made the occasion festive rather than businesslike. To drive home the point further, the pretty girls at the Tata pavilion were dressed in Indian attire, unlike the other pavilions where Western skirts were the norm. Cleverly gauging the mood that this car would be the showstopper at the Auto Expo, the organizers dressed up in smart sherwanis as well. And there, under the spotlight in the centre, stood the Tata car.

The Auto Expo is a biennial event that is held in the vast Pragati Maidan grounds. Pragati means 'progress' in Hindi— the arrival of the Tata car in January 1998 ensured that the grounds lived true to their name. An indigenously built Indian car was not merely a symbol of progress but an act of faith:

few people had ever imagined that India would make its own car. The minister of commerce and industry, the late Murasoli Maran, saw the car at the expo and immediately called it 'The Kohinoor of India'. Like the legendary Kohinoor diamond, the car sparkled, attracting huge crowds.

The car itself had not yet been christened, but seeing the five prototype vehicles on display, the guest columnist for Rediff.com, Veeresh Malik, wrote about the car: '"like Zen" would be the best description, except for the fact that, unlike Zen, it has an excellently roomy rear seat. Test drives, however, were out for the moment. For those of you wondering, yes, it is likely that TELCO [as Tata Motors was known then] will make, and sell, a world class car. It appears to be, frankly, like a cross between the Maruti Zen/Alto and the Mercedes Benz A-Class small car with cheaper specs.'

Vikram Sinha, who now heads the car manufacturing plant at Tata Motors, recalls being present at the unveiling. 'There was exceptional euphoria all over,' he says, and his eyes light up even today. 'There were endless queues to see India's first car, and I even met people who had come all the way from Mumbai just to take a look. What struck all of us was the feeling of patriotism and pride which flowed through that hall!'

Girish Wagh, who is now in the senior management team at Tata Motors, and who has played a key role in spearheading the development of the latest small car, Nano, was a young engineer in Tata Motors at that time. He recalls with pride that his father, who was a member of the Indica project team, was there at the auto show launch. 'My father called it one of the most fulfilling and satisfying days of his life,' he says, 'and that means everything to me.'

Patriotism, Pride and Courage

Cars have always been symbols of patriotism and pride. Famous auto brands such as Toyota, Rolls-Royce, Mercedes-Benz, Ford, Fiat and others have virtually been flag-bearers for their respective countries. Yet, in the early 1990s, India, despite having launched missiles and spacecraft, did not have a car it could call its own, a car that had been designed and produced within the country. In 1993, Ratan Tata, chairman of Tata Motors, addressed the Automotive Component Manufacturers' Association of India in New Delhi, and suggested the possibility of component and car manufacturers in India getting together to produce an 'Asian car'. His intent was to emulate the Japanese and deliver a project worthy of national pride.

It was a good time to launch a brave new effort, because the Indian government—headed by P.V. Narasimha Rao, along with able economist Manmohan Singh as finance minister—had announced a slew of liberalization measures just a couple of years earlier, designed to take the country into a fast-paced growth trajectory, and eventually into the league of First World nations. History has shown that cars are often an engine of rapid economic growth all over the world.

Speaking on the reaction to this address, Ratan Tata said, several years later:

> Needless to say, there was considerable criticism and cynicism about my suggestion. In the absence of a positive reaction, I decided that if we were not going to do this as a collaborative national effort, Tata Motors would undertake the lead effort.

In 1995, we formally undertook a programme to develop a new Indian car. Two types of reactions were forthcoming at that stage: one was that we were being very brave but, the other, which came more often, was that we were being very foolish.

Both of these extreme reactions stemmed from two facts. First, Tata Motors had achieved fame and success as a maker of trucks and commercial vehicles—it had never made cars. Second, the venture was very expensive, entailing investments of around Rs 1700 crore, and could make or break the company's fortunes. Of course, this was not the first time that the chairman of the Tata Group was being faced with intense cynicism regarding a pioneering new venture, or being labelled 'foolish' for pursuing a courageous dream.

In a classic example of history repeating itself, here is a relatively ancient anecdote that took place more than ninety years ago, as told in *The Creation of Wealth*. This was when Jamsetji Tata, then chairman of the Tata Group, was pursuing steel manufacturing for the first time. Till 1903, India had never made its own steel. Lala recounts: '[When he heard about the Tata Steel venture] the Chief Commissioner for the Indian Railways, Sir Frederick Upcott, said—Do you mean to say that the Tatas propose to make steel rails to British specifications? Why, I will undertake to eat every pound of steel rail they succeed in making.'

A few years later, when the Tata Group had made a big success of the steel venture, Mr Dorab Tata, who succeeded Jamsetji as chairman, commented dryly, 'If Sir Frederick had carried out his undertaking, he would have had some slight indigestion.'

This time, while there was once again no dearth of naysayers who refused to believe in an Indian car, there are no reports of any of them offering to eat the car. Since the Indica weighs 995 kg and contains over 2000 steel components, it may have caused severe indigestion. On the other hand, many sceptics would have fit into this car with ease, because Ratan Tata was clear that the new car had to provide ample space for the typical Indian family. In his own words:

> We started out to design an Indian car from scratch. We felt that the Ambassador, much as it is maligned, is the ideal size for the travelling Indian public. So we decided to design a car with the internal volume of an Ambassador, the size of a Maruti Zen, and ease of entering and exiting, particularly for the rear seats. We thought of pricing it close to the Maruti 800, which is a very successful car, and adding the economy of diesel. Finally, we packaged this into a contemporary design.

These famous words became a clarion call to everyone in Tata Motors, as the company commenced the exciting and arduous journey of building India's first indigenous car, rising to the chairman's challenge.

Futuristic Design

The first task was to finalize a design concept for the car, because most other things flow from the basic design. Ratan Tata led this path-breaking effort from the front. In this effort, he was perhaps also propelled by his own deep and abiding love for aesthetics and design.

The only cars that were seen in India those days were the Ambassador, the Premier Padmini and the Maruti 800. The original concepts for these cars had been created several years ago in countries outside India. None of these vehicles could be described as having exciting, contemporary designs. The first two vehicles looked and felt prehistoric when compared with the sleek modern cars one saw in Hollywood movies, but these dinosaurs stubbornly refused to go into extinction. Occasionally, a few beautiful but expensive imported cars also made it to Indian roads, and received envious glances from people who could never even think of owning or travelling in one of them.

If the Indica had to be world class, its design had to be comparable with the best in Europe and America. It had to be contemporary, appealing and so distinctive that it would sweep Indians off their feet. This task was assigned to the company's designers at the Engineering Research Centre located in Pune, commonly called the ERC. The designs were then refined and finalized in association with the famous Turin-based design house, I.DE.A. The ERC is a formidable facility, with a brilliant team of engineers. The designing process was completely automated at the centre using computer-aided design (CAD) and computer-aided manufacturing (CAM) stations, a novelty in those years. Tata Motors invested a massive sum of over Rs 120 crore on 225 CAD stations for its 340 engineers to work on.

When I visited the ERC during the writing of this book, it was buzzing with activity, as it must also have been during those early days of the Indica development, beginning in 1995. Several smart young design engineers in the company got the rare opportunity to work on India's first car project. One of them was Ravindra Rajhans, a member of the core development team. Rajhans had graduated with a master's degree in industrial design from one of India's most reputed engineering colleges, the Indian Institute of Technology (IIT), Mumbai. He had earlier worked on the styling of a light commercial vehicle (LCV) called the Tata 709, and also on the Tata Safari, a sports utility vehicle (SUV) that appeared to be a crossover between an LCV and a car. When he was asked to join the Indica team, he says he nearly fell off his chair.

> Those were heady days. We had the privilege of presenting our sketches and designs directly to our chairman, Ratan Tata. We were told that the design of the car would be developed by us, and finalized in collaboration with I.DE.A., a design house in Turin, Italy.
>
> I remember a meeting in Pune during September 1995, where some of us asked the chairman—'Sir, why are we going to Italy? Can't we do the design here, entirely in our own facilities in Pune?'
>
> His answer told us what the quest for world class meant. Mr Tata looked us in the eye, and said—'I believe totally in our own capabilities. But when we visit motor shows abroad, we see the great strides which global car companies have made, the excellent designs they have already launched in Europe and other Western countries. Our effort should be to leapfrog into the future. For this to happen we should work in the design environment of Europe, where the design ethos is well ahead of India. Then we can hope for a car which is ahead of its time.'

Turin was, therefore, a perfect choice; it is the design capital for the stylish Italian car industry, housing firms such as I.DE.A., and the headquarters of brands such as Fiat, Lancia and Alfa Romeo. It is also breathtakingly beautiful, surrounded on the western and northern fronts by the majestic snow-clad Alps. Natural beauty has always been a source of inspiration for intensely creative people such as designers.

Meanwhile, back home in Pune, a mammoth exercise in creativity and execution was under way: over 3800 components, 700-plus dies and 4000 fixtures for the Indica were being designed. These parts were also being simultaneously tested and validated, which was made possible by CAD systems that had been installed just in time for this project. In fact, paper drawings were done away with completely, which was an achievement in its own right.

Between Pune and Turin, the engineers at Tata Motors had to address several complicated design challenges. The car had to rise to Ratan Tata's challenge, and provide the space large enough for an Indian family. A typical Indian family has five or six people—husband and wife, two children and one or two grandparents who live in the same home. On long drives, the family also travels with a significant amount of luggage. One must not forget to mention here that this luggage will include tasty, freshly cooked home-made or local food. From personal experience, I can confidently say that this matter of food receives a lot of attention while planning a car journey.

For a product from the house of Tatas, which enjoys the trust of millions of Indians, safety had to be a zero-compromise feature. A colleague who lives in Europe, once commented on the car driving experience in India: 'How do you drive safely on roads where, on one side, autorickshaws are zipping by madly like Formula 1 cars, while on the other side cows are ambling as if the roads were their favourite meadows?'

The engine, which is at the heart of the car, had to provide excellent performance and mileage. Here, the Tata Motors team worked with Le Moteur Moderne (LMM), France, for engine testing and evaluation. The transmission system was designed entirely in-house, adding new capabilities to a company that had no background in cars. Accelerated learning became the mantra of the hour in all areas, simply because there was no in-house expertise of manufacturing cars to fall back on.

When the first prototype of the Indica was unveiled several months later, in some secrecy within Tata Motors, it was clear that this design effort had succeeded brilliantly. Everyone agreed that here was a car clearly ahead of its time; it looked very distinctive compared to other Indian cars of that period, and had an unmistakable international appeal. Everyone agreed that the car offered incredible space when compared to any vehicle of similar class. And the Indica met global crash test standards with ease. But at its heart it was an Indian car.

Rajhans recounts an interesting 'Indianness' story from his days in Turin.

I remember the day the first design prototype of the Indica was finally ready, and it looked so beautiful. My colleague and I, who were deeply involved in the design effort, wanted to celebrate the occasion before shipping the prototype car to India. In Italy, they celebrate with champagne. But we were so proud of the Indianness of the car that we wanted to celebrate with a puja (prayer) to God Almighty, for having guided us in making our design so successful, so wonderful. To perform this traditional puja ceremony, we needed a coconut, haldi (turmeric) and kumkum (vermilion). But where do you find these in a place like Turin? We roamed virtually every road and cobbled street of Turin for an entire day, hunting for these three essential items. It was difficult, but we eventually found them. We conducted our Indian puja and left the broken coconut in the car, as a symbol of the Almighty's blessings.

I am told that our colleagues back in India were most surprised to find the coconut, when they opened the shipment and unveiled the car!

Everyone who saw the prototype car remembers their first reaction even today.

Girish Wagh says that he first saw the purplish-blue Indica when he strolled into the prototype shop on some other work. 'Wow, what a wonderful new Toyota car!' was his first thought. It was only when he got closer that he realized it was not another vehicle from the Japanese Zen master of cars, but the new Tata car.

Some other reactions from the Tata Motors shop floor were equally euphoric. 'The first sight of the car was a "wow" moment for us. This was breakthrough styling, and we knew it as soon as we saw it!'

'The final design was chosen by Mr Tata, out of a few shortlisted concepts. We fell in love with it; we knew instinctively that we were backing a winning horse.'

Components of a World-Class Car

Even as the design concept was constantly being refined in collaboration with I.DE.A, work had also commenced on another big area—manufacturing or sourcing of components and vendor development.

The 3885 discrete designed components of the car now had to be locally developed and manufactured, either by Tata Motors or by capable vendors. Quick decisions were taken on which parts would be made internally and which outsourced. Either way, most of these were being made for the first time ever within the country. Global car companies such as Ford Motors and General Motors have grown on the back of strong vendor partners such as Visteon and Delphi, built over several decades. Tata Motors, on the other hand, did not have a vendor base for car parts. It had to develop this vendor community from scratch. It had to ensure that vendors met the global quality standards required, making it a task of Herculean proportions.

One man who recalls this vividly is Dilip Huddar, who is now the general manager of strategic sourcing for the company. He was a key member of the Indica ancillary development team.

> Our mandate was to develop the supplier base for the new car. A special team was created, called SQIG—the Supplier Quality Improvement Group. We were told that over 500 cars would be made per day.
>
> Until then, our plant was manufacturing around 100 trucks or Sumo vehicles per day, so this was a huge mindset shift! We used to begin work at 6.30 a.m. to make this possible, and end the day pleasantly exhausted but never before midnight. There was so much to do and so little time. This was such a large and prestigious investment for us; we were determined to make it happen really well.

Another member of this team was Atul Chandrakant Bhate, who heads product development for the cars business today. He had joined Tata Motors in 1992, fresh from graduate school where he had studied mechanical engineering.

'I was terribly excited when I was selected for the cars project. On the very first day, we were told that we would be given intensive training by an expert named A.J. Agnew, on development of parts for cars. The message was very clear—this is a different ball game from trucks and commercial vehicles.'

A.J. Agnew had been worldwide director of supplier quality at the Cummins Engineering Corporation in the USA. It was clear that the Tata Group was sparing no effort to ensure a world-class car. Agnew made it clear that everything had to be aligned perfectly with the final quality of the car, which is what mattered to people buying the vehicle. He emphasized that even the smallest compromises were not to be accepted, that tolerances had to be very strict and narrow. A detailed thirteen-step quality improvement programme was immediately put in place.

Dilip Huddar recalls: 'Our vendors were initially shocked that they had to carry out so many big quality improvements. Some of them began asking, why invest so much money into improving quality when Indian consumers will be happy with less? We had to convince them that Indian consumers deserved more, and Indica was determined to provide them the best.'

Nonetheless, several entrepreneurs were very keen to supply parts to the first Indian car. This was a matter of real pride for them. Some of them had even unofficially seen drawings of the new car, which had fuelled their interest further. They were now insistent that they would supply, and they did. In the midst of such exciting work with individual vendors, yet another major development was pioneered by the company, which would soon become instrumental to the future of the Indian car industry. Tata

Motors decided to float a holding company for manufacturing car components, called Tata AutoComp Systems Limited. This company then formed joint ventures with global giants for specific components, thus bringing the best possible expertise into the country from different parts of the globe.

A joint venture with Johnson Controls of the United States was established to produce car seats. A partnership with Ficosa of Spain produced rear-view mirrors. Radiators were produced by a third company that was formed in collaboration with Toyo, Japan. These are some of the countless partnerships that Tata Motors formed with various global players. These joint venture companies, under the umbrella of Tata AutoComp Systems, today supply to a range of Indian and global vehicle brands, including Tata Motors, Ashok Leyland, BMW, Mercedes-Benz, Ford, Mahindra & Mahindra and Honda. Indica had not merely given India its first indigenous car; it also helped establish in the country a global supply chain for cars!

Apart from Tata AutoComp Systems, more than 300 vendors were developed, which supplied over 1000 high-quality parts. In turn, this created a stream of 12,000 jobs. Nearly 98 per cent of all parts used in the Indica were made in India, an amazing statistic for a country that had never before made its own car.

'We created the entire sheet metal vendor fraternity around Pune,' says Atul Bhate. 'Sheet metal used in cars is large and voluminous, so vendors had to be close to our car manufacturing plant.'

He goes on to add:

Many vendors have also gained handsomely from the Indica car project. Several thousand jobs have been created at their

173

units, and small fledgling factories have now become large, profitable enterprises with revenues running into hundreds of crores of rupees. They are today large, sophisticated units catering to an array of brands. Some of them are listed on the stock exchange, and even have styling studios of their own!

Where Should the Indica Be Manufactured?

While components were being developed, thought was also being given to where the Indica would eventually be manufactured, bringing together thousands of these components and shaping them into a complete car.

As the story goes, the team at Tata Motors Pune had initially concluded that Indica cars should be manufactured inside a building called the E-block. This is a set of buildings located within the existing commercial vehicles factory of the company, where trucks and LCVs had been manufactured for several years. The managers who came to this conclusion were also ready with all supporting details and charts, and felt their decision was the most efficient approach. Then, Ratan Tata visited the plant and discussed the subject. He is reported to have asked for a pair of binoculars, which were duly given to him. Clutching these binoculars, he walked up to the terrace of this block and surveyed the surrounding areas. Standing there, he saw the barren land, over six acres large, adjoining the existing factory.

'That is where our cars will be manufactured,' he said, pointing to this vast tract of land. The need for a large, independent manufacturing unit for cars was proven right by several events that followed: the huge launch orders received for the Indica, the manufacture of other new cars such as the Indigo and Vista that were launched by the company in the following years and, of course, the rapid growth of the Indian car market.

'We thought of a unit for making Indica cars. He visualized a large, full-fledged car business that would transform the company. That was the difference,' says a senior manager, recalling this incident.

The Car Manufacturing Facility

But what about the car manufacturing facility itself? A new manufacturing unit can cost around $2 billion, or even more—a huge amount that could have broken the company's back or even rendered the project a non-starter. Here, again, Ratan Tata and his core team at Tata Motors took a road less travelled, and it made all the difference.

Here is Ratan Tata's description of how it all transpired:

Very often, in developing a car abroad, the cost of development is about US$800 million [approximately Rs 3400 crore] and the cost of manufacturing facilities is around $2 billion [approximately Rs 8500 crore]. In comparison, the Indica project cost us $400 million.

Looking for an inexpensive manufacturing facility, we found a disused Nissan Plant in Australia. It was run for fifteen minutes every day only to keep the hydraulics and pneumatics in working order. It was offered for sale and we paid about Rs 100 crore for it—barely one-fifth to one-sixth of what we would have had to pay for a new plant. Our engineers dismantled the plant, all 14,800 tonnes of machinery, and shipped it to India in some 600-odd containers, facilitating the construction of the plant in

Pune. This itself was a challenge, as it had never been done before. There were nagging doubts about whether we could dismantle an entire car plant and rebuild it. So, we tagged and identified the parts, then took them apart and rebuilt the plant as we went ahead. Of course, we added considerable new equipment to make the plant self-contained.

You would need over two lakh adult human beings to reach a weight of 14,800 tonnes! In addition to shipping this huge weight across two distant continents, every part had to be carefully taken apart, so that it could be put back together. This Herculean task was accomplished within six months, and over just sixteen shipments. What could have been a nightmarish effort was made to look effortless because of the determination and rigorous effort of the entire team.

Robots and the Indica

Apart from the Nissan factory that was rebuilt in India, the manufacturing facilities for the Indica comprise five different areas: the engine shop, where engines for the car are made; the transmission shop, where the gearboxes and gear transmission systems are made; the press and welding shop, where some parts are pressed into shape and then welded together; the paint shop, where the parts are painted; and the final assembly shop, where the entire car is assembled.

These shop floors are a delight to visit because they are a picture of the latest technology at work. They are normally buzzing with a constant stream of systematic activity, with hundreds of parts being made, transported, stored and stitched together.

When I walked through these buildings, I was also struck by how large they were, stretching almost endlessly. The senior engineers nodded. 'Yes,' they said. 'The assembly shop alone is more than half a kilometre long. Walking was taking too much time. So we began using bicycles to move through the shop floors.' Thus was created the unusual sight of young men bicycling within shop floors where India's first car was being created. With such distances being covered every day on foot or bicycle, no wonder these engineers look so fit and healthy.

The welding shop is an impressive place that gives a view of the huge technology leap made by the Tata Group; it is a veritable 'hall of robots'. It resembles a scene from a science fiction movie or an Isaac Asimov novel, with giant robots effortlessly picking up large car parts such as doors or fenders, handing them over to other robots that weld the parts, and cars that are in various stages of completion moving along fully automated pathways. At some points, multiple robots work together on complex manufacturing operations. There are over 450 robots in this single hall, so you will find more than one whichever way you turn.

All across the hall, a million sparks fly as welding guns completely operated by robots and computers carve out shapes on the cars. The reddish-coloured robots are many times the size of a human being; their ability to lift such large pieces of heavy metal with ease is an accurate demonstration of their incredible strength. A layman like me felt at ease only because, being a science fiction buff, I believe in the first law of robotics (from Isaac Asimov). Every robot is designed to obey this law, which specifies that 'A robot may not injure a human being, or through inaction let a human being come to harm'!

The head of this welding shop and supreme commander of this army of robots is Abhijit Ghaisas, a soft-spoken engineer who walks with a certain sure-footedness and acknowledges greetings from several workers on the way.

'Robots are used here for welding because of their accuracy and repeatability. And of course because of ergonomic considerations, due to which human operators should not undertake some of these manually taxing tasks. We have three robotic lines here. And this is the first significant robotic line installed in India.'

The Indica Rolls Out

The final stage of manufacture is the assembly and testing of the cars. Today, the plant has the capacity to roll out 1000 shiny new Indicas per day, all ready to hit the road. But this was not the case when the voyage began.

Four shop floor operators who assembled the first Indica car found the going very challenging. Umesh Dhule, Sanjay Kurne, Kishore Jape and Uday Urankar were young lads in the Tata Motors factory back in 1998. Still on the right side of twenty, and hailing from the smaller towns of Maharashtra such as Kolhapur and Ahmednagar, they had just completed their apprenticeships. They had grown up in difficult economic circumstances, and spoke Hindi with the lilting Marathi accent that is common to this belt.

It took us eight full days to assemble the first Indica car. We did not even know the names of the parts, so how could we locate them properly? It took so long that we thought to ourselves, how are we ever going to meet consumer demand? We had heard that more than one lakh people had paid a lot of money and booked the Indica, and were now eagerly waiting for their car. Would we disappoint them?

We told our college friends back home that we were making India's first car. They laughed at us, and they said—'How can we ever make a new car in our country? Cars like this are only made in America and Europe, not in India.'

This was unfortunately the prevailing mindset about India's capabilities. However, it must be stated that this perception stood somewhat modified when the same college friends heard that the Tata Group was behind this venture.

Goaded by a sense of urgency and a desire to fulfil consumers' orders without delay, the rate of manufacture increased rapidly from one car per day to fifty to 100. Today, a new Indica car emerges from the factory every fifty-six seconds. From eight days to fifty-six seconds, now that's a remarkable journey! A few interesting stories from this journey provide some insight into the company and its people, and some reasons why India's first car was delivered so well.

Ratan Tata used to visit the Indica manufacturing facilities quite often. On one such early visit, he promptly noticed operators fixing the rear strut of the car manually. The operator would have to bend up and down 600 times to complete this operation on 300 cars each day. Ratan Tata called his managers immediately. 'How can we expect our men to do this throughout their lives? Surely it will damage their health. We must provide an automation solution, on priority.' The engineering department, amidst all its hectic schedules, rose to the occasion and developed a fixture to semi-automate the operation. This made life incredibly easier for the operators, who remember this fondly even today.

Two years later, the Indica was yet to deliver profits, and the company was staring at a massive loss because its commercial vehicles business was also facing a bad market. But, as the four operators recall, the company still gave them a very good wage increase that year. 'Frankly, we did not expect this. Neither were we in any position to demand such an increase in our salary, because we knew the poor financial situation. But the company was generous to us. That is why we love our company; that is why we give all our effort and energy to making these cars with all our heart.'

The operators also recall with pride that Ratan Tata has always been accessible to them, has routinely stopped by to exchange a few words whenever he visited, and has respected their ideas. In fact, many ideas from the shop floor were shared with the designers and accepted. Worker empowerment and involvement also led to a very good implementation of the production process, contributing to the final smooth rollout.

An identical sentiment is expressed several years later by a young graduate engineer, Neil Kamal Gupta, who supervises many of these operators in the Indica assembly plant today. 'Our senior management respects us; they take our ideas on board. P.M. Telang and Girish Wagh [who head the company and car business operations, respectively, in 2012] have full trust and faith in us, and that always makes me feel on top of the world! I want our latest Indicas to delight the customer completely, and I will do everything I can do to ensure that.'

With such splendid and committed effort, the first Indica rolled out from this assembly plant in the year 1999, just thirty-one months after development had commenced. Many people still vividly remember that it was a green Indica, a colour that is no longer manufactured today. Green was undoubtedly the right colour, given that the car was ready within three years, and it was now going full speed ahead. Everyone also remembers that Ratan Tata drove the first car, which was adorned with bright flowers. Many important dignitaries and the media were present for the celebrations.

After all, this was no ordinary vehicle. The name 'Indica' said it all: in ancient days, this was the name used by the mighty Greeks when they referred to India. Megasthenes, the Greek general and historian, wrote fascinating things about India in his famous book Indica. Now Indica was also the name by which the entire world would know India's equally exciting first car.

Here is a wishful piece of fictional modern history. If the Greek emperor Alexander the Great were alive and had visited India in these modern times, he would certainly have wanted to disembark from his famous horse, Bucephalus, and take a test drive of the Indica. He knew a thoroughbred steed when he saw one.

More Car Per Car

Tata Motors also focused a lot of attention on marketing the car to Indians in an unforgettable and compelling manner. Once again, this was a very different proposition from the company's existing business of selling trucks and commercial vehicles to fleet owners. To address the task, a separate strategic business unit and marketing organization was formed. It established new car dealerships and authorized service centres across the country.

Ratan Tata and his team thought that providing customers a new experience in car buying was an important part of giving them a new car. To establish these experiential standards, the company's own flagship dealership Concorde Motors was formed. Initially established as a joint venture with Jardine International Motors, it soon expanded to fourteen showrooms in key cities such as Bangalore, Mumbai and Delhi. It was kept lean but very responsive to consumer needs, offering virtually everything—sales, service and spares. Its objective was also to set the standards for dealerships across the country.

The big question now was: what should the central consumer proposition of Indica be? How should the car differentiate itself from other international brands? How best should this story be told to the common man, who had never before imagined an Indian car?

Rajiv Dube, the commercial head of this project, who later rose to become president of the passenger cars business of Tata Motors, embarked on this exciting journey with a newly created marketing team. An officer of the Tata Administrative Service, Rajiv had earlier worked in Ratan Tata's office, and therefore knew the chairman's mind well. He spearheaded his team to create one of the most memorable marketing campaigns ever in the history of the Indian cars industry.

Working closely with them in creating the winning advertisements for Indica was the reputed advertising agency Draft FCB+Ulka. Ambi Parameswaran, executive director and CEO of Draft FCB+Ulka, and also one of the country's foremost exponents in the discipline of marketing, recounts the story of how this was done:

For us, Indica was not just a car. It was India's first ambition to take on the world. It was Tata Motors' passion on wheels. A conscious decision was made right from day one, to assume a confident, aggressive approach, to instil a sense of pride in owning a world-class Indian car.

But first, we said, let us just show the car to consumers, and find out what they think, what they see as the most appealing features. So we parked the Indica at Worli (a prominent location in Mumbai), and we invited people to open the car and get in. There was tremendous response. Curiosity was so high; people just wanted to have a look at India's first car.

This was the same response that many managers of Tata Motors had experienced when they had taken the Indica for test drives on the roads of Pune. Ravindra Rajhans, the design engineer who had worked in Turin, narrates this story:

I was driving an Indica late at night, around 10.30 p.m., a few months before it was launched. It was dark, and suddenly I saw a motorcyclist chasing my car. I was very apprehensive, having heard a few terrifying stories about highway robberies and dacoities. I drove faster, but so did the motorcyclist behind me. Eventually he overtook me, parked in front of my car, and stopped me from going further. I was now seriously worried, and prepared for the worst.

The motorcyclist got down, along with a small boy who was on the pillion behind him. He said that his son wanted to see India's car—that was why he had been chasing me for so long. They saw the car and spent a few minutes appreciating it from all over. Then they thanked me and went away!

Apart from sheer curiosity, what did the hundreds of people who got into the Indica at Worli have to say? Listen to Parameswaran once again:

> People were pleasantly surprised that the Tata Group had made such a good-looking car. They asked us time and again, in Hindi—*'Yeh gaadi Tata banata hai? Yeh toh badi garv ki baat hai* [Does the Tata Group make this car? This is truly a matter of pride].'
>
> Everyone who opened the car was also delighted with the amount of space inside the vehicle. They kept saying there was far more space than they ever imagined.

These two insights—the hyper-curiosity it generated and the feedback that this was a great-looking car with lots of space inside it—were used to create the first advertisement campaign for the Indica.

Before the launch, a teaser advertisement further stoked curiosity, as it announced: 'India's most eagerly awaited car'. It created huge anticipation and lots of conversation around it. This tagline became so famous that it was picked up by the media and used extensively, even in unrelated areas. When India had a new prime minister soon after the launch of the Indica, this development was announced in newspapers as 'India's most eagerly awaited prime minister'!

However, even more famous and impactful than this teaser tagline was the next advertisement in the launch campaign. Building on the fact that the Indica offered more good looks, more space and more engine power, this advertisement described the vehicle as 'More car per car'.

This line was the result of inspired creative thinking, motivated by what consumers had said and several rounds of internal discussion with the Tata Motors team. Earlier lines such as 'The complete car' and the 'No compromise car' were discarded in favour of a line that exhibited attitude and total confidence. This was a perfect example of a resurgent India taking on the world. 'More car per car' became a phrase on everyone's lips soon after these advertisements appeared in newspapers and on hoardings across the country. In the final analysis, the line 'More car per car' was perhaps so successful because it was a perfect summation of Ratan Tata's clarion call, which had driven the entire Indica project from start to finish: 'A car with the internal volume of an Ambassador, the size of a Maruti Zen, the economy of diesel and pricing close to the Maruti 800.'

The Indica received a fabulous response, the best ever in India's history till the time. The car garnered 1,15,000 'fully paid' bookings within eight days of its launch. This was many multiples more than the bookings obtained by other international cars launched during the same period. This also showed the tremendous enthusiasm with which Indians had welcomed the first car they could call their very own. Within a few months, the Indica had notched up a commendable market share of more than 14 per cent in its segment.

The unbeatable pull of the Indica was acknowledged by the competition in many other ways. Just a few hours before the Indica was formally launched by Tata Motors at the vast Turf Club grounds in Mahalaxmi, Mumbai, the market leader Maruti Suzuki announced a significant drop of Rs 25,000 in the price of its flagship car, the Maruti 800. This was perhaps on Ratan Tata's mind when he went on stage that evening to present the Indica to the crème de la crème of the city. 'Thanks to Tata Motors,' he said, 'whichever car you choose to buy, you will now get more.'

The Agony and the Ecstasy

Many decades ago, the author Irving Stone titled his famous biography of Michaelangelo *The Agony and the Ecstasy*, in an attempt to capture the extreme emotional states that this genius experienced throughout his life. The same title best describes the first three years of the life of the Indica. Initially, there were several accolades, including record bookings that resulted in strong market shares. But dark clouds quickly gathered on this sunny horizon, and the company had to suddenly deal with a wave of unanticipated consumer complaints. Essentially, these revolved around several product quality issues that cropped up immediately after the launch.

Several consumers called in, complaining of high noise and vibration levels in the car. There were problems relating to winding the windows up and down. The performance of the engine came in for criticism. Word of mouth was quickly turning from highly positive to highly negative. Some Tata Motors veterans recall that this was not just a few isolated cases, but a flood of angry complaints. They wince, even today, when they speak about how customers turned violent at several locations. On the back of such negative feedback, sales of the Indica plummeted during the year 2000–01. Tata Motors announced its largest ever loss of Rs 500 crore during that year, and a few experts promptly blamed this loss on the failure of the Indica, and the company's decision to enter the passenger cars market.

The competition became hyperactive and began to write premature epitaphs for the Indica. A constant refrain heard in those days was that Tata Motors and Ratan Tata had made a big mistake in betting on an indigenously made car. And there is of course no dearth of condescending Western and Indian minds who never miss an opportunity to take potshots at India and other developing nations, which remain, in their minds, lands that are best suited to snake charmers, forests and elephants.

So was this the sad end of the Tata dream to make India's first car? Would it spell disaster for Tata Motors, which had made the back-breaking investment of Rs 1700 crore in the Indica project? Like the Titanic, had the Indica hit a fatal iceberg? Would it now drag down with it one of the most venerable companies of the Tata Group?

These were the heavy thoughts playing on everyone's mind when Ratan Tata called an emergency internal meeting at the Taj President Hotel in Mumbai, to take stock of the unfortunate situation and chart the way forward. Memories of that session are still vivid in the minds of many. Senior team members were encouraged by the chairman to vent their feelings of what had gone wrong, for as long as they wished. Many of them were sharply self-critical. It was clear that the huge financial loss had touched their souls, and the mounting customer complaints had hurt their pride. But, deep within, there was great resilience, undying hope, a commitment to make the venture a success.

Ratan Tata then steered the meeting in the direction of the improvements that were required. The conversation quickly converged on to what the team should address immediately. There was acknowledgement that some specific design flaws had to be rectified, even if this meant alterations in the basic design.

In the meanwhile, 'retrofit camps' were organized, where over 45,000 Indica cars were repaired, with forty-two parts being replaced entirely at the company's cost. Customer meets were held in every nook and cranny of the country, with a patient ear being given to every angry customer, and solutions being offered wherever possible. Senior managers from the marketing, design and manufacturing teams participated in these meets.

The Tata Motors team knew that pride and survival were simultaneously at stake. Of course the company had stumbled, and had to pull itself up very quickly. The chairman was leading this effort from the front, and all product changes necessary had to be implemented on a war-footing. There was some writing on the wall already, and there was little time left to erase it.

If courage is required to launch a breakthrough exploration to unknown lands, guts of steel are required to sustain the voyage when it runs into such rough seas. The team at Tata Motors proved itself equal to this daunting task. Working with Formula 1-like speed, they developed and implemented the required design changes. Vendors produced these altered parts. A new, robust Indica was ready by 2001, with key quality problems having been completely eliminated. It was launched in the market as Indica V2.

The word 'V2' announced the change loud and clear. This was also a technical-sounding suffix, therefore appropriate for a car. If Indica had been 'More car per car', the new Indica V2 was 'Even more car per car'. A fantastic television advertisement, which highlighted the product features of the new car, even as it re-emphasized the many positives of the original Indica, also helped build consumer conviction.

An interesting sidebar is worth mentioning here. This advertisement ended with a scene of several oriental-looking people, including the Indian actor Kelly Dorjee, bowing to the new Indica V2, in a tribute to its features. The thought was perhaps to depict the Indica V2 as being so good that even the Japanese, who are the masters of car-making, pay salute to it. Such exaggeration is of course the lifeblood of good advertising. However, the Korean car company Hyundai used this scene as a basis to launch a complaint against this ad film with the Advertising Standards' Association of India (ASCI). While this complaint was eventually not upheld, it highlights the impact the new Indica V2 and its advertisement campaign had on its competitors.

Indeed, the impact of the Indica V2 was extraordinary and immediate. It marked not merely the revival of the Indica but its brilliant success. It became the fastest-selling automobile in Indian history when it completed sales of 100,000 cars in less than eighteen months. Despite an overall economic slowdown in 2001, it recorded a growth of over 46 per cent in that year, whereas most international competitor brands clocked only single-digit growth during the same period. The market share zoomed to over 20 per cent during the year 2001–02.

The commercial success was accompanied by other accolades too. Ratings of the Indica V2 by the J.D. Power study, a fiercely independent and widely respected review of cars, jumped dramatically. The 2003 J.D. Power India customer satisfaction study ranked the Indica diesel car as the best in the operating costs category, even ahead of the market leader, Maruti 800. The reputed television programme *BBC Wheels* declared the Indica the 'best car in the Rs 3 lakh to Rs 5 lakh price category'.

The confidence was back, there were big smiles all around. There had been a rather large hiccup, but the team at Tata Motors had proven itself more than equal to it. India's first indigenously designed car had conclusively proven that it was an indisputable success.

More than the Indica

The Indica transformed Tata Motors from a successful truck maker to a modern automobile company, very sensitive to the pulse of consumers. A series of successful cars and SUVs have been launched by the company in the wake of the Indica, including the Indigo, the Vista, the Manza and the Aria. And, of course, the Nano, which has received universal acclaim as one of the most significant innovations in cars after the Ford Model T. Today, Tata Motors consistently occupies either the second or the third rank in the large Indian cars market, and the day is not far when (and here we borrow a phrase from Turin) it will aim to be Numero Uno.

The Indica also served as the perfect catalyst for transforming the car industry in India, ushering in the modern era, in the wake of economic liberalization in the country. It established the supply chain for the indigenous manufacture of cars by developing a range of competent vendors and collaborating with the best names in the world. This has served as a natural platform for many other global brands of cars to make their entry into India. It re-established Indian pride in engineering and manufacturing. By making India one of the few countries in the world to produce its own indigenously designed car, it emphasized that the engineering sector in the country was alive, vibrant and kicking.

It became a symbol of Indian prowess in developing world-class consumer products. The Indica was yet another pioneering venture by the Tata Group, going where no Indian company had gone before.

The Heart of Courage

I often wonder: where does such great courage come from? Does it come from deep within outstanding individuals and teams, as they pursue their passions and dreams? Does it emerge from a very strong sense of duty to the country, to society or, in a more limited sense, even to one's family? Or does it simply come from fearlessness, which often lends itself generously to a noble purpose?

Here is what Ratan Tata has to say about the Indica, the spirit and the heart of courage: 'I think we were more brave than foolish actually. Over the years, TELCO had introduced a series of products that took to the Indian roads, competed with Japanese products when those were introduced, and found their rightful place in the country.' He was referring here to commercial vehicles made by the company, such as the successful 407 and 709 series, as well as crossover vehicles such as the Tata Estate, Sierra, Sumo and Safari.

'In addition, I had faith in TELCO's engineers.' His belief in the company's engineers, particularly the 300-odd young engineers who were raring to go, was an important starting point for embarking on the voyage of the Indica.

'Can we do something that has never been done before? I would like to believe that it can be done. We can make it happen; we just need to make sure that we do it.'

'It is important, particularly for the younger people in India, to believe in what we are doing and that we can do much more. I hope the younger generation will take India to new heights, which I am sure they can. They need to believe in and recognize the potential of their own capabilities.'

The Road Ahead

Fourteen years after the Indica was launched, there are still many big challenges ahead of the Tata Motors cars business. Competition from large international brands with deep pockets and global resources has only got tougher. Achieving larger scale is even more critical today to keep costs low. Consumers have become more demanding, and ensuring world-class quality of products and services is essential. However, for a company that successfully created India's first car, taking a path that was so different, refreshing and challenging, this will only create multiple springboards for many more acts of courage.

Extracted from *Tata Log* by Harish Bhat

Chapter 12

Taj Hotels

One fine evening in the late 1890s, Jamsetji Tata, founder of the Tata Group, and a doyen of Indian industry, accompanied a foreign guest to a hotel in south Bombay. He was told at the entrance that while his guest was permitted, he could not enter the hotel. He was shown a board which read, 'Dogs and Indians not allowed.' Enraged, he vowed to build his own hotel, so luxurious and superlative in standards that others would pale into insignificance. To match international standards, he hired a European architect, someone from France or Italy. After a lot of effort, the architect started the project. A few months into the construction, he went back to his continent for an extended leave. Upon his return, he was aghast to see the hotel building constructed in the wrong direction. The front entrance was on Merry Weather Road near Colaba Causeway, and the rear faced the majestic Arabian Sea. His most precious project was ruined and he did not have the courage to show his face to the patron, Jamsetji. So heartbroken was he that he went to the top floor of the hotel building still under construction, and jumped to his death!

When I grew up in Bombay, these were the kinds of stories that we were regaled with every time we passed by the grand Taj Mahal Palace Hotel at Apollo Bunder. These stories sounded so much larger than life that they fascinated my childlike mind. Alas, these are only legends with no truth in them! Over the last 115 years of its existence, the Taj story has been captured in over ninety national and international travelogues and bestsellers. Dozens of researchers have studied its history, architecture and evolution. Most of them have documented the real stories behind the ideation, construction and existence of one of Mumbai's finest landmarks. Let's take a look at the real stories of why Jamsetji initiated the construction of the hotel. One reason was that in spite of being one of the most important trade destinations, even in British India, Bombay did not have any hotels of an international standard. So, when repeated comments were made about this evident insufficiency, Jamsetji said, 'I will build one.' He had intense pride and affection for Bombay, and wanted to give back something that would be cherished forever by its citizens. In fact, so great was his passion that the money spent for the construction of the Taj (over Rs 20 lakh) was not from Tata Sons, but from his personal funds.

On 1 November 1889, he bought the lease of two and half acres of reclaimed land near the harbour. The construction began in 1900.[1] The mythical story of the European architect who committed suicide has also been disproved by the original drawings of the Taj found in the Bombay University library. They were signed by Raosaheb Sitaram Khaderao Vaidya, a Hindu engineer, and his assistant, D.N. Mirza, a Parsi.[2] After Vaidya's death in 1900, W.A. Chambers completed the project. All of them had worked with Frederick William Stevens, an English architectural engineer who was the mastermind behind the designs of the Victoria Terminus and the Municipal Corporation Building, landmark locations in Bombay's multi-century heritage. Now for the story about the entrance of the hotel. It was meant to be on the Colaba Causeway side for three reasons. First, the carriages bringing elite guests to the hotel would have an easy entrance because the parking space was closer to the western side of the hotel. Secondly, the U-shaped wings of the hotel aimed at capturing the afternoon breeze that blew in from the Back Bay rather than the harbour side. Lastly, Jamsetji wanted the majority of the guests to have rooms overlooking the sea. So visionary were his plans that he even purchased two islands near Uran so that guests at the Taj could use them for picnics![3]

The Taj's greatest memory lies in the fact that it was inaugurated in the lifetime of its founder. On 16 December 1903, an ailing Jamsetji presided over its inauguration. The construction was still in progress. However, the first wing with two complete floors welcomed seventeen guests that day. It was a culmination of his two-year-long efforts, when he went all over the world to shop for his dream hotel—electrical machinery from Dusseldorf, chandeliers from Berlin, fans from USA, and the first spun steel pillars from the Paris Exhibition, where the Eiffel Tower had been constructed only in the previous decade. The architecture was a blend of Moorish domes, Florentine Renaissance, and Oriental and Rajput styles. The hotel boasted of its own power plant with electricity and a carbon dioxide gas ice machine plant that provided refrigeration and helped cool the suites. These were among the very first anywhere in India.[4] When Jamsetji breathed his last the subsequent year in Europe, the Taj, literally meaning 'crown', had begun its journey of shining as a jewel in Bombay's firmament.

The Journey from the Taj Hotel to the Taj Brand

Why do I write so much about just one of the 100 hotels belonging to the Indian Hotels Company Limited (IHCL)[5] across sixty-three locations in India, North America, the United Kingdom, Africa, the Middle East, Malaysia, Sri Lanka, the Maldives, Bhutan and Nepal? It's because of the historic role it played. For seventy of the 115 years of its existence, the Taj Bombay was the only property of IHCL. During these seven decades, it witnessed many a milestone. While it became the first choice of maharajas across India and royalty and heads of state from across the world whenever they visited Bombay, it also got converted into a 600-bed 'hospital' during the First World War.[6] In November 1933, the Harbour Bar at the Taj was India's first air-conditioned bar. Interestingly, it was the first bar in Bombay and had Licence No. 1. When the government first imposed alcohol prohibition in 1939, the Taj slipped into losses for the first time. It soon recovered as army men packed its rooms during the Second World War. Some time in the early 1960s, J.R.D. Tata, then chairman of Tata Sons, briefly flirted with the idea of selling the hotel as it wasn't doing well enough. However, he soon changed his mind. One of the reasons was the advent of jumbo jets which convinced him of the tremendous potential the hotel held for the future of tourism in Bombay. The other reason was Colonel Leslie Sawheny, Dorabji Tata's brother-in-law, who took charge of the hotel and literally turned it around in a decade, physically[7] and financially. Among his trusted aides was Ajit Baburao Kerkar, recruited in London as assistant catering manager in 1962.[8] By 1970, JRD made Kerkar the managing director of Indian Hotels. He shared JRD's vision and was given immense freedom to achieve it. Over the next two decades, with abundant autonomy and authority, Kerkar expanded IHCL's footprint from a single hotel to many dozens across India. The first addition was the Taj Mahal Tower, constructed just next to the main hotel in 1972. In the same year, the Oberoi Towers inaugurated their property at Nariman Point, just 2 kilometres away. Such was the bonhomie displayed by the Taj that it published print ads which read, 'Taj welcomes its friend to share the fortunes of this great city.'[9]

The Darkest Cloud, with a Thick, Silver Lining

Articles, reports, books, documentaries and films have been made elaborating what happened during those fateful sixty-eight hours that began at 8.30 p.m. on 26 November 2008 (often referred to as 26/11), when ten terrorists representing the Pakistani extremist outfit Lashkar-e-Taiba (LeT),[10] travelled over 500 miles through the Arabian Sea from Karachi to Mumbai, and laid siege in parts of India's 'maximum city' with nearly 2 crore residents. The attack, planned with military precision, killed 166 innocent people and injured over 300. Amid resounding gunfire in the heart of south Mumbai, Operation Black Tornado, led by the National Security Guards (NSG) of the Government of India, neutralized the terrorists. Nine of the terrorists were killed, and one, Mohammed Ajmal Kasab, was caught alive in a Skoda car near Chowpatty Beach while trying to escape.

On most days, the Udyan Express from Bengaluru is delayed and arrives late at platform number 15 at the

Chhatrapati Shivaji Terminus (CST) Station at 9.30 p.m. If it had arrived at the same time on 26 November 2008, I would have probably lost my dearest mother, returning from a pilgrimage. Fortunately, the train was on time, and she was out of the station only thirty minutes before Ajmal Kasab and his fellow terrorist Ismail Khan mercilessly sprayed bullets at hundreds of commuters on the CST platform—men, women and children. They killed fifty-eight people. Around the same time, in another part of the city, our five-decade-old neighbours, Sevantilal and Sarla Parekh's only son, Sunil, and his wife, Reshma, had just entered the restaurant Tiffin of the Oberoi-Trident Hotel for a dinner meeting. Over thirty-six hours later, we received the tragic news that they were among the nine guests who were cruelly shot dead by two terrorists at the Trident. Their daughters, Anandita and Arundhati, were aged just twelve and eight then.

Of all the places targeted in Mumbai, the one where the fight with the terrorists lasted the longest was at the Taj Mahal Palace Hotel. Like the Opera House to Sydney and the Eiffel Tower to Paris, for over 115 years the Taj has been a prominent symbol of Mumbai. Even before the Gateway of India[11] was built in 1924, the hotel was the most outstanding structure on the Bombay coastline. In attacking the Taj and trying to destroy its century-old heritage wing, especially the historic dome, LeT wanted to leave a visible scar on the success story of India Inc. that was epitomized by one of the oldest institutions synonymous with Mumbai and its history. Over 1200 guests and 600 employees were inside the hotel for functions as diverse as a high-profile wedding reception, a Bohra Muslim wedding, Unilever CEOs Global Meet with thirty senior leaders from Unilever worldwide, and two other corporate meetings. The

Indian, Chinese, Japanese—indeed all restaurants—were full that Wednesday evening, when the first gunshots were heard.

The natural question then is how did the final number of casualties (guests and employees included) remain as low as thirty-one? With 1800 vulnerable people, and four terrorists loaded with the latest ammunition, the fatalities could have been ten to twenty times that number! The primary reason for this was the employees of the Taj, who went way beyond the call of duty to save as many guests as possible. Krishna Kumar remarked that all employees knew the exit routes. However, it was beyond his comprehension that in spite of that, not a single employee gave in to the natural survival instinct and left the premises. Karambir called them the real heroes of the Taj. Even before the NSG commandos could formulate a strategy to safely evacuate the guests from the premises, the employees had used their prudence and ensured that they were in safe areas, until help arrived.

Chef Hemant Oberoi's valiant team formed a human chain to protect 60-70 guests while escorting them from Wasabi, the Japanese restaurant, down the spiral steps into the kitchen, and out. Thomas Varghese (head waiter), Vijay Banja (executive chef), Hemant Talim, Kaizad Kamdin and Zaheen Mateen (chefs) and Rajan Kamble (engineer), employees serving the hotel in different capacities for many decades, voluntarily faced the line of fire while evacuating guests through the exit routes of the labyrinthine Taj. They laid down their lives by blocking the gunmen's path, and were spewed with bullets from those vengeful weapons. Mallika Jagad, the twenty-four-year-old banquet manager for the Unilever event, and her team, used their extraordinary presence of mind, switched off the lights and bolted the doors of the banquet room on the second floor of the hotel where the event was on. For over a dozen hours, she and her team took care of the guests who were ducking and squatting below the tables. Her team provided water and napkins from time to time for over ten hours. Finally, in the early hours of the morning, they were rescued by the fire crew through the windows. Amit Peshave, the twenty-seven-year-old manager of Aquarius, the Taj's 24/7 poolside cafe, had by instinct found his way out of the hotel's transformer room, from where another door opened out into Merry Weather Road, to the street on Colaba. However, his conscience tugged at him, and he came back to save thirty-one diners at the Shamiana restaurant. He was miraculously saved even though a grenade exploded close to him.[12] The telephone operators risked their lives but continued to hold the fort in the control room to ensure that the guests in various rooms within the hotel received information and instructions in real time.

Who can forget Karambir Kang, the forty-year-old GM of the Taj? His heroic leadership of the hotel not only got it the Best Overseas Business Hotel Award,[13] but also universal appreciation for making the best possible efforts to save the lives of thousands of guests, even when his own family, wife Neeti and sons Uday and Samar, were getting asphyxiated on the sixth floor of the Taj. In our conversation he recalled, 'You know, at that time, we didn't know the magnitude of the attack, and the number of gunmen. Were they four or ten? But in spite of that, in the given circumstances, we just took the right decisions with whatever knowledge we had. We all felt responsible for each other and for our guests. It's not that somebody was telling them to do whatever they did. But, independently, in different pockets of the hotel, they all acted the same way. It was remarkable.' He believed that what happened that day was a tangible expression of the employees' belief that the Taj was their family. The place had given them livelihood, made their lives, educated their kids, and enabled them to build their homes. 'The Taj is like a temple. It's revered by the staff,' he told me. Even in adversity, the employees stood by the company ideals and ethos.

Given the details already in the public domain, there is little scope for further elaboration on what happened during those three days inside and outside the Taj. The important questions from an organizational perspective are: What did the Taj do after the massacre? What were the reasons for which Taj employees behaved the way they did during those horrific hours, even risking their lives? What are the lessons that other corporations can learn from the events that unfolded on 26/11? I asked Raymond Bickson, who was himself stuck inside his office for nearly sixteen hours, 'What was the reason for the Taj employees' behaviour that day?'

'The reason my people created those human chains and essentially put themselves in between the terrorists and the guests was that they considered this hotel as their home. You cannot come to my house and you cannot harm my guests because they are my family. It was a direct manifestation of the Indian philosophy that the guest is God,' he said.

H.N. Shrinivas, the then senior vice president of human resources at IHCL, described the hapless scene outside the Taj. The terrorists were inside the hotel, the higher floors of the heritage wing were ablaze, and constant gunshots were being heard. Ratan Tata, Krishna Kumar, and other senior people from the company were standing helplessly on the pavements outside, not knowing what was going on inside or how many people had been killed. It was a horrendous feeling. Hundreds of employees from other shifts had flocked to the venue and were squatting on nearby roads. The police had laid siege around the hotel. In such a scenario, instead of lamenting the loss, Shrinivas's team took the traumatized employees sitting expressionless on the pavements to the nearby Holy Name High School, and requested the priest to permit them to use the hall, to which he kindly consented. Batch by batch, morning, afternoon, night, the next day morning, afternoon and night, his team continued to interact with employees and console them. Within a few days, employee assistance centres were set up in ten locations across Mumbai, each with two post-trauma counsellors, a medical doctor, a car, a van and two drivers. Details of Taj employees in each of those areas were prepared and they were brought to those centres along with family members. Shrinivas and his team explained to them what had happened, encouraged them that the Taj would once again bounce back from this rare tragedy, assured them that their jobs were not lost, and that they should unitedly fight the situation. 'All this spontaneously happened in the first fortnight. In those days, we hardly slept,' he recalled.

At another venue, Deepa was sitting in a 'war room', a crisis and emergency microsite that was put together for handling everything from lost baggage to finding people, and providing minute-to-minute updates on what was happening. 'It was a best practice in terms of how a microsite could have been used,' she said. At that time, a lot of requests for help were coming in from people in hospitals, whom the Taj was paying for. There were some people who had nobody to pay their bills. There was this dilemma as to whether the patient was connected to the tragedy at the Taj in any way. At that time, Krishna Kumar walked in with a message from Ratan Tata that the Taj should not distinguish while helping people, whether security forces, police, fire service, hotel employees, guests of the Taj or general public, whether killed or wounded. Tata had decided to form a trust which would pay for everybody injured anywhere in the city during 26/11.

Not only then but for the future too, for those affected by natural or man-made calamities, the Taj Public Service Welfare Trust was announced on 15 December 2008, only seventeen days after the disaster. Besides IHCL, Sir Dorabji Tata Trust[14] and Sir Ratan Tata Trust[15] committed a significant initial contribution to the newly formed trust. Ratan Tata himself was a part of the board of trustees that included Krishna Kumar and Raymond Bickson, among others.[16] Tata instructed the team to go to every hospital where the injured were being treated. If the hospital hadn't taken care of the bills, the Taj would do the needful, irrespective of whether the person was injured at CST or the Trident-Oberoi. Even hawkers and street vendors, who were injured during the attack, were taken care of.[17] Deepa emphasized that it was a part of the Tata culture to go beyond the ordinary and contribute. The staff witnessed the company's reaction being in total alignment with their sacrifice in the larger cause of human welfare.

Besides a number of other relief measures, the company decided that families of Taj employees who died during the attack would be paid their deceased members' salaries for the rest of their lives, as well as all medical benefits and education for dependents up to the age of twenty-four. Within a week of the attack, Ratan Tata wanted to meet the family members of all deceased and injured employees. They were flown into Mumbai for the meeting.[18] During the gathering, the wife of Thomas Varghese, a forty-nine-year-old waiter at the Taj, who came in between the terrorists and guests and took the bullets on himself, spoke to Tata. She said, 'My husband died for a cause and will always remain a role model for me and my children. I never knew I was living with such a great man for the past twenty years. All I want from my children is that they too should practise these values, stand tall in their lives and acquit themselves creditably before God Almighty. Practising those values is far more important than whatever money you are planning to give as a settlement.' For the first time, in decades, in full public view, Ratan Tata's eyes welled up. Recalling those moments, Shrinivas said, 'Interacting with the families, we realized that designations mean nothing. There are such great people in such simple positions. It is because of them that there is goodness in society.'

'We may have been knocked down, but not out,' Ratan Tata avowed. To communicate a message resonating this spirit, the Taj ran a three-part communication campaign 'Taj Forever', which aimed at healing, moving forward and communicating to the world that 'Taj is forever'. The first part emphasized defiance. 'It really hurt us that our flagship hotel was targeted. We were so emotional about it, and that was the message we tried to communicate by publishing defiant messages,' Deepa shared. The second part of the campaign contained healing messages to people who were injured and affected through this tragedy. The final part of the campaign emphasized that the hotel was renovated and the Taj was once again ready to welcome its guests. It was a common resolve that the Tower wing should be opened in record time. Within just three weeks of the attacks, it did reopen. It even went ahead with other planned events for December 2008 including launching the Vivanta by Taj in Bangalore, the Pashan Garh Lodge Resort in Panna (Madhya Pradesh) and the Taj Club House Chennai.[19]

The message to the world was that the Taj was not going to be bogged down by such acts of cowardice.

The weekend before the Taj was reopened, a staff-only programme was organized where spiritual leaders from all major faiths conducted prayers and healing rituals. For forty-five minutes, the names of all 1700 employees of the Taj Mumbai were read out to appreciate the unity with which they stood behind the company. 'Just to hear all our names echo in that hall was so reaffirming. It united us in a way that went deeper than the usual team-building programmes,' reminisced Bickson. The next day, 1000 people, including guests, friends and family, applauded continuously for fifteen minutes, tears streaming down many faces, as the 540 Taj employees who were on duty on the night of 26/11 strode proudly through the lobby on a red carpet.[20] They were the real heroes of a real adventure—the game called life. To share their solidarity with the families of those who had lost their loved ones, the Taj placed a memorial in the lobby, with the names of all thirty-one victims. It was a humble tribute to their bravery and sacrifice in the darkest hour of the hotel's history. It was a memorial for future generations to commemorate the ideals the departed employees had placed before the company and its guests. In the months following the attack, the employees at the Taj Hotels were trained in advanced security, safety and disaster management in collaboration with a specialized Israeli company.[21] Traditionally, hospitality and security don't go hand in hand. Yet, what 9/11 did to the American airline industry, 26/11 did to the Indian hospitality industry. The fun and freedom of going to a five-star hotel and relaxing in a cocoon was lost in large measure for good.

On reflection, there are three lessons that companies and institutions can learn from the Taj in light of their response to the terror attack. Firstly, the way in which Ratan Tata and the entire management of the Taj handled the aftermath. It was the most mature response to an event of that magnitude. What left most people spellbound was that within three weeks of the attack, the Taj once again opened its doors to welcome guests. It was symbolic of defiance coupled with courage. Secondly, the response towards their employees. Typically, when two-thirds of a hotel is closed down, any organization would retrench some part of its employee base, as large as 1800 people. However, the Taj didn't. Not a single person was retrenched. Instead, the period was used to further train the employees and raise service levels. Many were transferred to other Taj properties so that they could continue their good work. Lastly, the manner in which the Tatas decided to take care of the families of the deceased, not only the employees but also from the public at large, was beyond normal expectations. These lessons go far beyond a win-win solution or strategy. They were far beyond any economic or even ethical considerations. They were in the realm of morality and bordered upon spirituality. An acknowledgement to this came from a person no less than the President of USA. In 2010, during his historic ten-day visit to India, President Barack Obama chose the Taj as his residence in Mumbai to show his solidarity with the victims of 26/11. During the visit, he said, 'To those who have asked whether this is intended to send a message, my answer is simply, absolutely!'[22]

Extracted from *Win-Win Corporations: The Indian Way of Shaping Successful Strategies* by Shashank Shah

Chapter 13

Indian Institute of Science

The Presidency Universities of Bombay, Madras and Calcutta had given India its first graduates with a background of western education. In 1889, Lord Reay, Bombay's popular governor, said in a convocation address that education could no longer develop if universities remained purely examining bodies. He called for 'real universities which will give fresh impulse to learning, to research, to criticism, which will inspire reverence and impart strength and self-reliance to future generations.'

Such advanced learning was not available in India, so in 1892 Jamsetji endowed a fund for the higher education abroad of deserving students. Some of India's early engineers, surgeons, physicians, educationists, barristers and ICS officials benefitted from the endowment. Once the Indian Civil Service was thrown open to Indians, Jamsetji was especially keen that deserving Indian students should take advantage of it. (Some years later, in 1924, it was calculated that one out of every five Indian ICS officials had been a J.N. Tata Scholar). But the progress of the early years was too slow for Jamsetji's liking.

Writing to Lord Reay on 17 November 1896, he told the Governor of Bombay that 'no more . . . fruitful results, can be provided than (by) a national system of education.' He continued: 'The efficiency of general education must depend, in the last resort, on the efficiency of the highest university education.' In September 1898, Jamsetji announced an offer that was to astonish men of his day. He decided to set aside fourteen of his buildings and four landed properties in Bombay for an endowment to establish a university of science. His donation was worth Rs 30 lakh in those days, equal to over Rs 10 crore of today. It was half his wealth. The other half he left to his two sons.

His offer fetching an interest then of Rs 1.25 lakh a year was hailed in many quarters, but some of his fellow Parsis regretted that the wealth of the community was being diverted to a scheme from which few Parsis would benefit, when such wealth of the community could be used to give clothes, food, medical facilities and housing to Parsis in need. In reply to them, Jamsetji, in an interview, spelt out his views on philanthropy:

> There is one kind of charity common enough among us, and which is certainly a good thing, though I do not think it the best thing we can have. It is that patchwork philanthropy which clothes the ragged, feeds the poor, and heals the sick and halts. I am far from decrying the noble spirit which seeks to help a poor or suffering fellow-being. But charities of the hospital and poor asylum kind are comparatively more common and fashionable among us Parsis. What advances a nation or community is not so much to prop up its weakest and most helpless members as to lift up the best

and most gifted so as to make them of the greatest service to the country. I prefer this constructive philanthropy which seeks to educate and develop the faculties of the best of our young men.

The proposal of Jamsetji was presented to the new viceroy, Lord Curzon, in 1898, the day after his arrival in India. The proposal was put to him by a deputation led by the vice chancellor of the Bombay University. Typical of Jamsetji, he did not say much on the occasion himself but let the vice chancellor, Mr Justice Candy, and others do the talking. Curzon was lukewarm, and had two major doubts about the scheme. The first was whether qualified Indians would be forthcoming for such advanced scientific training. Secondly, whether there would be employment opportunities for them in a country that had no industries worth the name.

To report on Jamsetji's scheme, the Secretary of State for India requested the Royal Society of England to send out an eminent scientist. The Royal Society selected Professor William Ramsay, the discoverer of rare gases (including helium and neon), who was later to be awarded the Nobel Prize. After a quick tour of the country in ten weeks Ramsay reported that Bangalore was a suitable site for such an institution. On Curzon's doubt whether the qualified students would come to the institute to be trained in scientific methods, Ramsay recommended liberal scholarships. Ramsay also indicated certain industries that could be developed in India. Later Curzon appointed a committee, consisting of the principal of the Roorkee Engineering College, Colonel J. Clibborn, and Professor David Orme Masson of Melbourne University to draw up 'a less ambitious plan' susceptible to expansion according to circumstances. The Clibborn-Masson Committee recommended Roorkee as a suitable area.

Meanwhile, Curzon was writing to the Secretary of State for India, Lord Hamilton, on 26 June 1901:

> We are endeavouring to save Tata's scheme from the shipwreck which his ambitions and Ramsay's exaggerated ideas threatened it, and are asking the Committee (Clibborn-Masson's) to consider and submit a scheme under which the annual expenditure will be limited to £10,000; £2,000 of which will be provided annually by the Government of India for ten years.

It may be mentioned that Jamsetji's endowment alone provided £8,000 (Rs 1,25,000) a year. Curzon also wrote to Hamilton that his government would propose to create the institution on a more modest scale and then if Jamsetji declined it, the responsibility for destroying the scheme would be upon Jamsetji Tata and 'we shall escape the odium which would have been fully bestowed upon us.'

Jamsetji had hoped 'that corporations, the native chiefs, sardars' will gradually see their way to bountifully help such an institution. For this reason he insisted that his own name should not be attached to the institute. The Maharaja of Mysore did come forward with a generous offer of 371 acres of land in Bangalore for the institute, a gift of Rs 5 lakh for construction and a recurring grant of Rs 50,000 a year. But no other source of revenue came forward. The Curzon government was taking its own time and was concentrating on cutting down and controlling the scheme. Did Curzon comprehend fully that what Jamsetji was after was not just a university of science but a new 'national system of education'? According to the original plan proposed by Jamsetji, the university was 'destined to promote original investigations in all branches of learning and to utilize them for the benefit of India.'[1]

The original plan by Jamsetji included: scientific and technological education; medical and sanitary education, including research in bacteriology; and studies in philosophy and education (including methods of education), ethics and psychology, Indian history and archaeology, statistics and economics and comparative philology.

The canvas that Jamsetji was working on was too vast for his contemporaries to fathom, far less to accept. The largesse he had given for the institute was from his private account. To increase the regular income of the institute, he wished to levy and lay aside a certain commission from his business. His colleagues in business opposed him. Jamsetji must have felt hurt. Though he could have pushed through his idea, he graciously bowed to the desire of his colleagues and restricted his endowment to his personal wealth. Attacked by some co-religionists, denied co-operation from those he had inducted into his business, confronted with an arrogant viceroy who could not understand the greatness of the giver or of his gift, any other man than Jamsetji would have withdrawn the offer. In fact the British reckoned that he would. Lord Hamilton, who had sympathy for Jamsetji, wrote to Lord Curzon in 1903: 'My impression is that Tata will drop his scheme and devote a certain proportion of his endowment to practical purposes in connection with electricity or the development of the iron industry.' But Jamsetji was not easily deflected from the accomplishment of his purpose. In

1904, Jamsetji added a codicil to his will urging his two sons not to use this money set aside for the university. If need be, he requested they add to the university from the wealth he was leaving them. While the scheme was still being considered and a provisional committee was looking into it, Jamsetji died on 19 May 1904. Perhaps *The Times of India* was thinking of him and Lord Curzon when it wrote the following day that Jamsetji's 'sturdy strength of character prevented him from fawning on any man however great, for he was great in his own way, greater than most men realized'.

In the year 1905, when Lord Curzon was on leave in Bexhill, he finally gave the green light to Dorab Tata, by agreeing that the government would meet half the cost. Dorab, who was educated at Caius College, Cambridge, and knew quite a bit about the West, wrote to a friend in India that year: 'One thing is certain. India is not ripe for the institute and I doubt very much that Britain is ripe.' In prophetic tones he continued:

> If we make the effort to give India what she might have we shall have achieved something, even if the institute, when established, fails to answer our expectations. It is thus, I think, that the beginnings of all great reforms take place. The man who sows never gathers the fruit. It is left to somebody else at some remote date to make the tree bear fruit. All that the man who sows ought to be content with is that the tree should remain alive so that at some future date another might give it the right treatment and make it bear fruit.

'To give India what she might have' became the lodestar of the House.

A director was speedily appointed in 1906. When the vesting order came from the Government of India in May 1909, it was generously worded. The order which vested in trust the properties endowed by Jamsetji Tata, spoke positively of the enlightened promoter and donor. The order stated that 'the Governor-General in Council has no desire to associate himself intimately with the actual administration of the institute, or to claim a determining voice in the settlement of the lines of research to be followed and the methods of instructions to be employed.' The powers were vested in a Senate, a Court and a Council of the institute. To the credit of the British government and its successor governments of independent India, this autonomy of the institute and its academic freedom have been honoured. From its inception the institute is a tripartite venture of Tatas, the Government of India and the Government of Mysore (now Karnataka). In view of its national importance the Government of India bears the expenses.

The institute opened in 1911 with three major departments of General and Applied Chemistry, Electro-technology Chemistry and Organic Chemistry. Chemistry, which now is divided into several disciplines, in those days covered a very vast field. In the 1940s and 1950s aeronautical engineering, high voltage engineering, internal combustion engineering and several others were added. Today the institute has over thirty departments.[2]

The Indian Institute of Science, Bangalore, has occupied a pre-eminent position in national life. The Council of Scientific and Industrial Research (CSIR) was established in New Delhi only in 1942 and India then set on the path of opening national research laboratories in the late 1940s and 1950s. The first Indian Institute of Technology opened at Kharagpur in 1950. Bombay,

Madras, Kanpur and Delhi IITs came up by 1961. In the early years the institute at Bangalore focused on utilizing indigenous materials to benefit industry. The Mysore Soap Factory and Sandalwood Oil Factory were among the early beneficiaries. The origin of the hydrogenation industry can be traced to the work done by the Department of Organic Chemistry.

Like Tata Steel in Jamshedpur, the Indian Institute of Science in Bangalore has spawned many children. The Central Food and Technological Research Institute in Mysore, the Lac Research Institute of Ranchi and the National Aeronautical Laboratory in Bangalore are the direct offshoots of the Institute of Science. The institute also provided the nuclei for the National Chemical Laboratory and the National Metallurgical Laboratory. The alumni of the institute provided the backbone for our national laboratories and the CSIR.

Distinguished names in science and industry have been closely associated with the institute. The industrial genius Sir M. Visvesvaraya was closely associated with the management of the institute for three decades. Nobel Prize winner Dr C.V. Raman was director of the institute for four years and did his important work on crystals and spectroscopy at the institute where he was the head of the department of physics for many years. Professor Max Born specially came to see the work being done by Dr Raman at the institute. Dr Homi Bhabha did his pioneering work on cosmic rays during the years of World War II and Lord Wavell visited the institute as viceroy mainly to see Dr Bhabha's work. Also at the institute was Dr Vikram Sarabhai, who succeeded Dr Bhabha as the head of India's atomic energy programme. Dr Satish Dhawan, who became director of the institute in 1961, was later selected to concurrently head the Indian Space Research Organization.

When asked what are the distinguishing characteristics of the institute, its director, Dr C.N.R. Rao,[3] says, 'For success in intellectual endeavour the first requisite is freedom. We are the most free in India; truly autonomous. Once a member joins a faculty nobody bothers him, be he a lecturer or professor. Rank does not come in the way of a person's work. People are able to devote themselves to their research. Any staff member can get seed money for his research.'

Professor M.N. Srinivasan of the Faculty of Mechanical Engineering observes, 'The three distinguishing characteristics of the institute are: it has created an environment for research, it promotes creativity and witnesses intense activity. At all hours of the night several students—including ladies—can be walking to their laboratory through the campus to carry out their research and get computer time. All courses are taught in the framework of research and even for a Master's degree about half the time is given for laboratory research.'

The total student strength of the institute is 1,400 inclusive of students doing research work and course work. The faculty strength of the institute is 440.[4] In numbers, its pool of research workers is the largest in any educational research institution and next only to the Bhabha Atomic Research Centre (BARC). Staff and students of the Indian Institute of Science produce a thousand research papers a year. About one of every ten members of the Indian Academy of Sciences is a member of the institute. India's top scientific award is the Bhatnagar Prize and the Indian Institute of Science has by far the largest number of awardees. Its research projects and funding is the largest of any academic institute in India—Rs 15 crore recurring grant and another Rs 6 to Rs 8 crore for identified research projects.[5] Most of the research is in the frontier fields and in the practical application of science to industry, to rural development, to low-cost housing. For example, the institute has invented a wood-burning stove made of mud with an efficiency in the range of 35/45 per cent which is being used in the whole state of Karnataka leading to a 65 per cent saving in firewood. The entire poly-silicon technology of the country has sprung from the institute. The institute has contributed to the progress of India's aeronautical and space programme and assists private industry with consultancy.

The institute has a wind tunnel and a water tunnel. The wind tunnel, for example, tested the ability of the second Howrah Bridge to withstand pressures.

The institute's Continuing Education Programme upgrades the knowledge of 3,000 scientists and technologists annually.

The reason why Jamsetji Tata did not want to give his name to the institute was spelt out by him in a letter proposing his scheme to Lord Reay in 1896. Jamsetji said:

> It is my firm belief that corporations, native chiefs, sardars and native gentry will gradually see their way to bountifully help such an institution . . . I want no title for myself, nor do I wish my name attached to anything. The national movement ought to bear a national name and every separate benefactor might be at ease as far as I am concerned that his endowment won't bear a name subsidiary to any.

That is why he did not want his name to be lent to the institute.

In the Platinum Jubilee year, the institute decided to build a modern auditorium with a seminar complex and name it the J.N. Tata Auditorium.

Tatas continue to be represented on the Court, the Council and the Finance Committee which are the decision-making bodies. According to its former registrar S.S. Prabhu, 'Tatas have provided, at crucial times, the healing touch.'

When Jamsetji Tata dreamt of the institute, he wrote:

> The objects of the institute shall be to provide for advance instruction and to conduct original investigations into all branches of knowledge . . . likely to promote the material and industrial welfare of India.

His dream has been fulfilled.

Extracted from *The Creation of Wealth: The Tatas from the 19th to the 21st Century* by R.M. Lala

Chapter 14

Tata Finance

Legend has it that, nearly 500 years ago, on 31 October 1517, a letter signed by the German monk Martin Luther was pinned to a church door in Wittenberg. It had far-reaching consequences in the Christian world.

Nearer home, and much closer in time, a letter dated 12 April 2001, written by a person who called himself Shankar Sharma, reached the desks of several important and influential people in Mumbai. It had a similar dramatic impact in the Tata world.

The recipients of the letter included the directors of Tata Finance Limited, India's stock market regulator, the Securities and Exchange Board of India (SEBI), and several leading newspapers. It levelled several allegations against Tata Finance and its erstwhile managing director, Dilip Pendse. It charged that a prospectus issued by the company, for a rights issue of preference shares, contained falsified information. It also alleged that a fraud had been committed in the company.

Most people who read the news, including myself, reacted with disbelief. How could a document issued by a Tata organization contain false information? Was it conceivable that a major fraud could be committed by a managing director of a company that was part of this respected corporate house? This is the shocking tale of how things went terribly wrong in Tata Finance. It is also the story of how the Tata Group acknowledged and dealt with the whole affair, establishing, in the process, new standards of corporate governance in the country.

Dreaming Big

Tata Finance Limited was a company with big ambitions. It had grown rapidly in the late 1990s, branching out into several areas of financial services. These included the hire and purchase of commercial vehicles and the financing of cars and consumer durables. The company accepted fixed deposits from members of the public, providing them a good rate of interest in return. It was planning to enter merchant banking, securities trading and other financial advisory services. Dilip Pendse, the managing director, was the chief architect of many of these plans.

Within the company there were dreams of glitzy offices that would rival those in the financial nerve centres of Canary Wharf, London and Wall Street, New York. A magnificent building in the Fort office district of Mumbai had been purchased, to serve as the future corporate headquarters. Young team members would often imagine how this building would eventually look—with handsome brass plates, busily flashing trading screens and hundreds of consumers walking in every day to buy or sell stock, invest in deposits or apply for loans. This would be a one-stop financial services shop, the likes of which India had never seen before.

Tata Finance also established a housing finance subsidiary, called Tata Home Finance Limited. It structured tie-ups with leading manufacturers and marketers of vehicles. A joint venture company was formed for rendering foreign exchange services in India. The company was clearly exploring growth through multiple opportunities including strategic alliances, and it was pursuing this with speed.

Grand events symbolized these ambitions quite vividly. One occasion was the launch of Tata Finance-American Express co-branded credit cards that was held on the terrace of the exclusive Chambers in the Taj Mahal Hotel at Mumbai, in December 2000. In full view of the splendid Gateway of India, the sparkling Arabian Sea and the majestic central dome of the Taj, the card was launched with much fanfare as yet another milestone on the company's pathway to heaven.

No one could have imagined that beneath this bright visage flowed a murky current. Until the moment the shocking letter from the man who called himself Shankar Sharma arrived.

Shock, Introspection and Determination

In an article on this subject published by Tata Group Publications, appropriately titled 'Grime and Salvation', Ishaat Hussain, finance director of Tata Sons, says: 'That letter alerted us, and further investigations revealed that there had indeed been some serious irregularities.' He goes on to add, 'We were all taken aback.'

After an initial denial of the allegations by the Tata Finance management, it soon became clear that the letter was a case where smoke indicated a raging fire. The predominant mood in Bombay House, headquarters of the Tata Group, was one of dismay and anger at what had happened, but there was also a realization that dealing with this matter openly and transparently was the most important thing to do now. There was a sense of extreme urgency, and Tata Finance occupied the mind space of several senior directors of Tata Sons.

Meanwhile, it became painfully clear that Tata Finance had become almost insolvent. It had borrowings of about Rs 2700 crore, a huge figure by any standard. Of this, Rs 875 crore represented money belonging to four lakh small depositors. For many of these depositors, these were savings of an entire lifetime, funds kept aside for retirements, children's marriages and medical emergencies. They had trusted Tata Finance with these funds primarily because of the Tata name and, now, Tata Finance was not in a position to repay these depositors. There could not have been a worse moment in the history of a financial corporation.

How had this situation come to pass? The detailed events leading to this debacle can perhaps be the subject of an entire book, filled with many plots and sub-plots. Yet the key story, which was rapidly unfolding, was as follows: Tata Finance, led by Dilip Pendse, had lent approximately Rs 525 crore to some of its own subsidiary companies and affiliates, including a company called Nishkalp. A large part of that money had been invested in the stock market, in scrips of poor and speculative quality. Later investigations by the company revealed that many of these stock transactions were carried out to secure personal profits. When these scrips came crashing down, the original investments vanished and only a gaping black hole remained, with nowhere to hide.

In the midst of this tense and unfortunate situation, the chairman of Tata Sons, Ratan Tata, clearly defined two principles which would guide action. First and foremost, the interests of every depositor would be fully protected, so that no one who had trusted the Tata name lost on account of these ill-advised actions by some members of the Tata Finance management. Second, a thorough investigation would be completed, so that the guilty could be legally pursued and punished.

Ishaat Hussain says in 'Grime and Salvation', 'Mr Tata recommended to the Tata Sons board that they stand behind the company and make available funds to meet all its financial commitments, and the board fully endorsed this.'

Magnitude and Speed of Response

Pause here for a moment, dear reader. Reflect on the fact that Tata Sons could have merely adhered to its limited legal responsibilities, rather than be determined to meet all the financial liabilities of Tata Finance. Also, consider that the quantum of funds required to do this was very significant. Arranging for such an amount at short notice posed challenges of feasibility, logistics and much else. Where would the funds come from? Who would be responsible for raising the full amount? How would the monies be returned to individual depositors across the length and breadth of the country, wherever required?

Yet, this was not merely the chosen path; it was the spontaneously chosen path. Having observed decision-making in the Tata Group for over two decades now, I am convinced that any option that did not meet these basic principles of honesty and fairness would have been peremptorily tossed into the dustbin. Therefore, the way forward was proposed and adopted quite unanimously.

On 25 July 2001, an extraordinary public statement was issued, candidly admitting that Tata Finance was in distress as a result of a fraud committed upon it, and the Tatas would ensure that no depositor lost any money.

The Tata Group, working through two holding companies, Tata Sons and Tata Industries, provided Tata Finance with cash and corporate guarantees amounting to Rs 615 crore. This was an unprecedented event in Indian corporate history. These funds would be available to repay all creditors, as and when required. So every depositor could sleep peacefully, knowing that his or her funds were absolutely safe.

The Non-Flying Helicopter

In the offices of Tata Finance, Ratan Tata's instructions infused fresh energy and life.

At a meeting held among key employees in the corporate headquarters, a clear decision was communicated: no depositor who wanted his money should ever be turned away, even for a single moment, without his money. Detailed plans were made to implement this decision, covering every town and every branch of Tata Finance across the country. The entire company was put into execution mode.

A small story illustrates the determination with which the team responded to the crisis. Everyone knew that if nervous depositors came to the offices of Tata Finance asking for their funds, a speedy response was critical. Therefore, it was even decided to keep a helicopter on standby so that funds could be transported quickly by air, if necessary. The team felt proud to be part of a Tata company, and wanted to ensure that people were not let down, whatever the cost or effort.

The helicopter was not used at all, though it may have added some excitement to these proceedings and also provided Indian television channels a few dramatic visuals. All these elaborate arrangements were rendered entirely redundant—such was the trust in the Tata name and the reassurance provided by the company, that only a handful of the four lakh small depositors withdrew their money. There was no run on the bank, not even the faint beginnings of one, despite the public statement and everyone knowing about the huge losses that had been incurred.

An investor named Luis De Menezes wrote to the Indian Express during those days, and a paragraph from his letter captures the prevailing sentiment well:

> Even after the scam [how former Managing Director Dilip Pendse helped run up huge losses], I have not thought of withdrawing my fixed deposit from there. At least for me, Tata Finance is the only trustworthy NBFC left in which I can deposit my money and have sound sleep. The culprits involved in this scam should be brought to book and also sued for tarnishing the Tata name.

I had myself held a fixed deposit in Tata Finance in those days, and the thought of withdrawing it did not even occur for a single moment, the simple reason being that I instinctively knew it would be absolutely safe, even though I wasn't privy to the discussions of those days.

Pursuing the Culprits

Getting to the bottom of the entire affair and bringing the culprits to book was the second principle that Ratan Tata had laid down for dealing with this episode. This was important in all such cases, not merely to resolve the issue at hand and to ensure that the guilty were punished but also to throw up important lessons and changes required for the future.

The episode of Nick Leeson, financial whiz-kid turned rogue trader at the Barings Bank, comes readily to mind. By indulging in unauthorized trades and hiding losses from his superiors who considered him a financial rock star, he lost an unbelievable sum of $1.3 billion. These losses were more than the entire capital and reserves of the bank, and therefore effectively wiped out a 230-year-old institution. Barings had been considered infallible and had served as bankers to the Queen herself. Now, it all came crumbling down. Leeson was arrested, extradited to Singapore where the crimes had been committed, and sentenced to six and half years in prison.

More importantly, the investigation of this collapse immediately threw up important lessons in internal controls, sound monitoring, risk assessment and risk management. Many international banks quickly took these lessons on board, and made the necessary changes in their processes and structures. These remedial actions are unlikely to entirely prevent all future attempts at fraud, since highly intelligent and equally crooked human beings will always find new ways to beat the best processes and controls. But the measures resulting from the investigation will certainly help reduce the probability of their occurrence.

In a similar fashion, Tata Finance launched its own investigation, and then moved forward to initiate legal action against those found guilty in the affair. Here is yet another excerpt from 'Grime and Salvation' that summarizes the steps that were then implemented expeditiously:

The internal team and external investigators also evaluated available documents and built up a paper trail. In the first week of August, based on legal advice from an eminent criminal lawyer and a report from an independent chartered accountant, Tata Finance and Tata Industries filed an FIR (first information report) with the Economic Offences Wing, Mumbai Police, against Mr Pendse and certain former Tata Finance employees.

But matters were not to end here.

'We moved the courts when the Mumbai Police filed a closure report with respect to our complaints,' says Mr Hussain.

'We took the stance that we will not let go the culprits. We moved the Bombay High Court and got the investigation transferred to the Central Bureau of Investigation. In the Supreme Court, too, our stand was vindicated. Six criminal complaints were filed in all, including three with the Delhi Police, and six complaints with SEBI for violation of various securities laws.

'Dilip Pendse was charge-sheeted in two complaints, and taken into judicial custody.'

These actions showcase the admirable resolve of the Tata Group, to deal firmly and summarily with any subversion of the value systems that Tata stands for. However, there were also some systemic errors and failures to be dealt with to guard against the recurrence of such episodes.

Matters of Corporate Governance

The eminent Irish novelist James Joyce once said, 'A man's errors are his portals of discovery.' Stepping through the unfortunate portals of the Tata Finance episode, the most obvious discovery is that no institution is above error or poor judgement, not even one as reputed as the Tata Group.

While the directors of Tata Finance resigned, taking constructive moral responsibility for this extraordinary lapse, many questions of governance remained to be addressed. Where had the checks and balances failed? Why had no whistle-blower come forward to reveal the fraud much earlier in the day? Why did they keep quiet, until the surfacing of the Shankar Sharma letter? Did the board of directors of Tata Finance discharge its responsibilities with the independence and oversight required of it?

Clearly, there were shortcomings in many of these areas of corporate governance, and therefore many lessons to be learnt. The Tata Group has, since then, put in place several processes to strengthen these systems of governance, which are the backbone of any institution. Some of these are statutory requirements, and others are crafted specifically by the Tata organization. Here are some important examples:

Chief financial officers of Tata enterprises now no longer report only to the managing directors of their respective companies. They also have a line of reporting to Bombay House, where the finance director of Tata Sons is based. This dual structure of reporting ensures not merely review of key data and financial information at multiple levels but also opens channels of communication that are invaluable to the governance process, at the seniormost levels of the organization.

Similarly, the chief internal auditor reports to the chairman of the Audit Committee of the board of directors, who is an independent director with expertise in matters of finance, accounting and controls. He is not aligned with the promoters and is not a member of the company's management either. This helps ensure sharp, expert and independent oversight of a critical watchdog function, which is charged with highlighting deviations and lapses.

The Tata Group has also put in place a written code to prevent insider trading. There is also a policy to encourage whistle-blowers to come forward and report ethical or other important concerns.

Boards of directors have also become much more accountable, not merely for performance but also for good governance. There is increasing consciousness that, at this high table, they are protectors of the company, its brand name and legacy. They have to shoulder an increasingly weighty burden on this front as companies become larger, wealthier, more complex and widespread in their operations.

These are good lessons arising from a particularly painful episode. But there is another area, even more important, that is essential to reflect on. It is the subject of values and culture, in ensuring good corporate governance.

Values and Integrity

Every institution has a set of publicly stated beliefs and value systems. These are put up on soft boards and notice boards in our offices, where we see them every day. But, as a human resources head in a large Tata company told me during the writing of this book, the truth is that every employee does not necessarily put into practice all these values. Companies have to live with this mix of people. Therefore, companies have to ensure that they spot the 100 per cent practitioners who truly believe in all these stated values, and rely on them to lead the organization. This is very important, because in moments of great temptation or crisis, these values are inevitably put to the test.

Noshir Soonawala, one of the most respected senior leaders in the Tata Group, emphasizes that the need to maintain values, principles and character at all levels is paramount. He points out that maintaining principles on every tier, in all dealings, across so many businesses and so many people will become even more challenging as the Tata Group continues to grow and expand dramatically. He views this as one of the foremost challenges for the future.

Here is how Ishaat Hussain sums up this challenge:

> Good governance is the lifeblood of every reputed organization. Of course this requires strong processes and vigilant boards of directors, but most importantly it requires professional integrity on the part of senior executives. We have to bear this in mind while selecting our chief executive officers, chief financial officers and their counterparts, in the future. If they are unscrupulous and, particularly, if they gang up together, they can drive coaches and horses through the system.

The Reincarnation of Tata Finance

The story of Tata Finance does not end here. At walking distance from Bombay House, in a stately looking building called One Forbes, are the elegant corporate offices of a relatively new company called Tata Capital. The company, established in September 2007, promises consumers that it will do just what is right for them. It offers a suite of financial services including consumer loans, investment services, commercial finance, investment banking, securities, travel and forex services, credit cards—in fact, products and services which are identical to the dreams that Tata Finance once had.

With strong systems of governance and decision-making, a vigilant senior management and board, the company is well on its way to making a big and positive impact in the world of finance. The decisions that the Tata Group implemented several years ago during the Tata Finance crisis are a strong foundation on which Tata Capital has now been built.

In the final analysis, public trust in the Tata brand has only been enhanced by the transparent, upright handling of that crisis. To err is human. It is the organization's response to an error committed, in one of the constituent parts in this case, that severely tests principles and character.

The Identity of Shankar Sharma

Finally, who is Shankar Sharma, the man who wrote the letter alleging that fraud had been committed in Tata Finance? Was he an outsider who had gained access to information, or was he an insider who wanted to alert the Tata Group and others to wrongdoings within the company?

More than a decade later, his identity remains unknown and mysterious. He perhaps had the best interests of the company at heart, and the corporate world will need many more people like him. His letter certainly made its impact. However, this story can be complete in all respects only after a conversation with him. So, I wonder, will he ever reveal himself?

Extracted from *Tata Log* by Harish Bhat

Chapter 15

Tata Trusts

'Trusteeship' was a by-product of the desire Jamsetji Tata and his sons had to tackle the needs of the nation. Their wider concern made them look beyond their business interests. For example, when Swami Vivekananda spoke of the rise of the ascetic spirit in the country, Jamsetji Tata (who had met him aboard a ship) wrote him in 1898 suggesting 'the establishment of monasteries for men dominated by this spirit, where they could devote their lives to the cultivation of sciences—natural and humanistic.' He offered to 'cheerfully defray all the expenses of publication' for a pamphlet by Vivekananda and doubtless would have financed a monastery or two.

Jamsetji Tata had a burning zeal to pitchfork his country among the great industrial nations of the world. His schemes for steel, hydroelectric power and the institute of science were geared to this one aim. So was his passion to train young Indians. In 1892 he started giving scholarships to deserving students for higher studies abroad. Jamsetji said: 'Though I can afford to give, I prefer to lend.' Thereby students, after they qualified, could return the loans and thus help others to go in for higher studies with the same funds.

Once the ranks of the Indian Civil Service were opened to Indians, Jamsetji was eager that enough Indians reached the highest ranks of administration. And a fair number of scholarships were awarded to ICS aspirants who had to travel to England. In 1924 it was calculated that out of every five Indian ICS officials, one was a Tata Scholar.

It is the measure of a man who lived ahead of his times that he pioneered higher education among women. The first name in his register for scholarships in 1892 was that of a lady medical doctor, Miss Freny K.R. Cama. She was loaned in those days Rs 10,000 which in terms of today's money is worth thirty times the amount. She returned as one of India's pioneer gynaecologists. In 1902 an agreement was signed with Krishnabai Kelavkar, who went on to become FRCS, Dublin. On a single page of the register of the J.N. Tata Endowment Fund for the period 1905 to 1909 appear the names of the following scholars: A.R. Dalal, who became director of Tata Sons and a member of the viceroy's executive council; J.C. Coyaji, later chief justice of the Bombay High Court; B.N. Rao, ICS who rose to be a judge of the International High Court at The Hague; Dr Jivraj N. Mehta, eminent physician and chief minister of Gujarat. Later scholars included nuclear scientist Dr Raja Ramanna, economist Dr V.K.R.V. Rao and the future President of India, K.R. Narayanan. The last three were also ministers in the Union Government.

The register bears brief interesting remarks on the candidates, occasionally on their travails and their performance. In 1915-16, S. Ranganathan stood third in the ICS examination. In the remarks column, alongside his name, the trust authorities solemnly note: 'All clothes stolen from his trunk at Marseilles. Fresh sum sanctioned by the trustees for new clothes.' A host of distinguished civil servants to be given study loans by the trust includes C.M. Trivedi, S. Bhoothalingam and V.T. Dehejia.

In one case both father and son have been Tata Scholars. In 1928 V.V. Narlikar was given a scholarship to study applied mathematics at Fitzwilliam House, Cambridge. In 1957 his son, J.V. Narlikar, was given a scholarship for the mathematical tripos at the same Fitzwilliam House. The Hoyle-Narlikar theory expounded at Cambridge was a product of this scholarship.

From 1977, as a tribute to the founder, some major companies of the Tata Group have made annual contributions to enable J.N. Tata Endowment to select a larger number of Tata Scholars and to augment the amount of the awards. For brilliant students it is not just a question of obtaining the finance needed for study abroad. There is a prestige attached to being 'a Tata Scholar' and on the strength of it many a scholar has gained admission in universities abroad. Currently about 2,000 apply. About 300 are called for the interview with a panel of experts in their course of study. They must qualify with conspicuous distinction throughout their career and be under twenty-seven years of age to be J.N. Tata Scholars. About 100 are selected each year. A decade later the numbers of those applying are 3,000, called for interview 600 and selected are up to 150.

Jamsetji was fortunate in his sons. His younger son, Sir Ratan Tata, sensed the importance of the work of Gopal Krishna Gokhale in India, and of the then little-known Mohandas Karamchand Gandhi in South Africa.

For a number of years Sir Ratan supported Gokhale with generous contributions. Able men renounced their ambitions to serve in Gokhale's Servants of India Society. On 19 October 1909, referring to Sir Ratan Tata's help to the society, Gokhale wrote of 'the deep gratitude I feel for your overwhelming generosity to my Society. There is no parallel to it anywhere in the country. I can only say that members of the Society will ever cherish your name as that of their greatest benefactor.'

Sir Ratan contributed to Gandhiji's campaign for racial equality in South Africa a sum of Rs 1,25,000—not a negligible amount for those days. Sir Ratan wanted the best institution in the world to do research into the causes of poverty and its alleviation. In the last six years of his life he gave each year £1,400 to the London School of Economics for this purpose. The trustees continued the donation some years after his death. It led to the establishment of the Sir Ratan Tata Department in 1912, now called the Department of Social Sciences at the school.[1]

In 1913, the London School of Economics advertised for applicants for a lecturer for the Ratan Tata Department. Only two applied. One was a young man called Clement Attlee and the other was called Hugh Dalton. The authorities 'after very careful consideration' selected C.R. Attlee for the post. Thirty-two years later Attlee became the Prime Minister of Britain, and Dr Hugh Dalton was to be a Chancellor of the Exchequer in the Attlee Cabinet. In 1947, as chance would have it, it was under Attlee's government that India was granted independence.

In *100 Great Modern Lives* edited by John Canning (Souvenir Press, London), in the galaxy of personalities only two Indians feature—Mohandas Karamchand Gandhi and

Jamsetji Tata. The chapter on Jamsetji Tata concludes with the paragraph: 'Probably no other family has ever contributed as much in the way of wise guidance, industrial development and advancing philanthropy to any country as the Tatas have to India, both before and since independence.'

Sir Ratan and Sir Dorab Tata established pioneering trusts geared to building the educational, social and scientific infrastructure of this nation. At a time when most charities were only communal in nature, the Sir Ratan Tata Trust (1918) and the Sir Dorabji Tata Trust (1932) established a precedent of being universal in their generosity. The Anjuman-i-Islam or a Hindu institution could lay as much claim on its resources as any Parsi charity could—and they did.

Sir Dorab was particularly clear on this point, mentioning in his deed of trust that 'without any distinction of place, nationality or creed', the trust should institute, maintain and support schools, educational institutes, hospitals and offer relief in cases of distress caused by natural disasters. He also stressed 'the advancement of learning in all its branches especially research work in connection with medical and industrial problems.'

The trustees of Sir Dorabji Tata Trust followed the example set by the founder of Tatas, Jamsetji Tata, who had planned the Indian Institute of Science in Bangalore as a pioneering institution to provide the country with the trained personnel needed to man its future factories and laboratories. In addition to giving grants liberally each year for the advancement of learning and the relief of distress caused by natural disasters such as floods or drought, the trustees established some major institutions of a pioneering character, like the Tata Institute of Social Sciences (1936), the Tata Memorial Centre for Cancer

Research and Treatment (1941), and the Tata Institute of Fundamental Research (1945), conceived by Dr Homi Bhabha, which became the cradle of India's atomic energy programme.

After an interval of twenty years, one of the trustees, Jamshed Bhabha, proposed that the resources of the trust which had hitherto been reserved for the fields of medicine, science and technology, should also be channelled into the area of the arts and humanities where there was a pressing need for a pioneering institution. Although music has for centuries been an indispensable part of the culture and civilization of India, it has no form of notation such as makes possible the preservation of western music in the form of printed music scores. Its survival has depended entirely on oral tradition and master-pupil links. This has been jeopardized in the last fifty years by the disappearance of old sources of patronage which had assured a source of livelihood for the great masters and teachers, and since the independence of India by the creation of new job opportunities in business and industry which tended to draw the brighter children of artistes away from traditional family vocations.

In 1966, by virtue of the support of J.R.D. Tata, the trustees adopted Jamshed Bhabha's project for a National Centre for the Performing Arts. In addition to a programme of large-scale archival recording of classical and folk music and the sustenance of the *Gurukula* (master-pupil) system through the medium of masterclasses, the centre has constructed India's first national theatre—the Tata Theatre. Since then the Jamshed Bhabha Theatre has opened.

In the decade of the 1980s Sir Dorabji Tata Trust has played a leading role in establishing the Centre for the Advancement of Philanthropy in Bombay, to assist the formation of new trusts and the functioning of the existing ones. The centre publishes its own journal, *Philanthropy*, the only one of its kind in India. The trust also conceived India's first helpline for drug addicts and assisted Kripa Foundation to launch it in Bombay. At the initiative of the trust the first directory of facilities available in an Indian city for the treatment and rehabilitation of drug addicts was compiled and published by the Tata Institute of Social Sciences.

Every few years Sir Dorabji Tata Trust has a tradition of setting up a major innovative project. Professor Rustom Choksi who had handled with distinction Sir Dorabji Tata Trust for four decades noted that:

> What distinguishes a Trust is not its ability to give or the extent or range of its giving but the character of its giving. It is important for a Trust to maintain its 'pioneering' character and this can only be done adequately where from time to time a Trust initiates and fosters new institutions and new types of service to society. For a great Trust the large project, carefully designed and executed, must always be a major objective. Even in the routine giving of grants and donations the Trust must constantly bear in mind the 'pioneering' factor.

In pursuance of this policy Sir Dorabji Tata Trust started in 1989 the National Institute of Advanced Studies with Dr Raja Ramanna, former chairman, Atomic Energy Commission, as its director.

Very often the two trusts of Sir Dorab and Sir Ratan move hand in hand. The Sir Ratan Tata Trust took the primary responsibility for erecting the J.N. Tata Memorial Centre at Navsari, giving the birthplace of Jamsetji a civic centre, an auditorium and a library. To the Sir Ratan Tata Trust's initial donation of Rs 25 lakh, the Sir Dorabji Tata Trust and a number of Tata companies happily joined in taking the figure to Rs 55 lakh. The industrial house of Mafatlal made a contribution of Rs 5 lakh for the gardens.

Sir Dorab Tata gave his trustees considerable latitude to take up new projects to meet changing situations.[2] Many of these earlier contributions were made in the 1930s and 1940s when the value of the rupee was ten to twenty-five times that of today.

The two trusts and their outreach reflect the different personalities of the two brothers. Sir Dorab, the elder brother, was a domineering and efficient industrial magnate. It was he who pioneered in bullock-carts the search for iron ore and built up the steel plant and other industrial ventures.

Sir Ratan Tata, as his photograph shows, was a sensitive and artistic personality, interested in paintings, sculpture, archaeology and the like. In his will he noted:

> If I leave no children, I give the rest or the residue of my property . . . for the advancement of education, learning and industry in all its branches including education in economy, sanitary science and art or for the relief of human suffering or for other works of public utility . . . Such work is not (to be) undertaken from a stereotyped point of view but from the point of view of fresh light that is thrown from day to day by the advance of science and philosophy on problems of human wellbeing.

Sir Ratan died in 1918 at the age of forty-eight, leaving behind his widow, Lady Navajbai Tata, who was to outlive him by forty-four years. The residue of his property amounted to Rs 81 lakh. Although the Sir Ratan Tata Trust has contributed significantly to the great institutes launched by the Sir Dorabji Tata Trust,

Sir Ratan had a very distinct personality of his own that reflected his sensitivity to the suffering of mankind. The Ratan Tata Industrial Institute is well known for providing women from lower income groups a framework for a decent livelihood.

The trust has spread itself out contributing generously to homes for the homeless, hospitals, outpatient dispensaries, village schools, blind schools and the like. The National Metallurgical Laboratory received the major grant of Rs 12 lakh from the Sir Ratan Tata Trust while the National Centre for the Performing Arts and the Tata Institute of Social Sciences have each received about Rs 10 lakh from it. Other beneficiaries have been the Indian Institute of Science at Bangalore, Delhi School of Economics and the Bombay University. Incidentally, Sir Ratan's art collection which included works by European masters, worth a fortune now, was donated to the Prince of Wales Museum, Bombay, where it is housed in a special wing along with the art collection of Sir Dorab Tata. The Tata collection was one of the first major gifts which enabled the museum to be launched, and Tatas have a representation on its board.

A distinctive aspect of these Tata trusts is that in recent years the Tata enterprises have undergirded the initiative of the Tata trusts as has happened with the National Centre for the Performing Arts.

There are other Tata trusts that have made their own contribution:

The Lady Tata Memorial Trust was started in 1932 by Sir Dorab Tata in memory of his wife, Lady Meherbai Tata, who died of leukaemia. In those days very few were engaged in leukaemia research and the Lady Tata Memorial Trust made its impact as an early comer on the world stage. The trust promotes research principally by means of international awards in addition to a fifth of its income being allotted for Indian awards. Its advisory committee in London has eminent European experts on its board. At a symposium on leukaemia held by Ciba in London in 1953, it was found that of the world experts who had assembled, more than a third had secured support from the trust at one stage or another in their career. It may be mentioned that this trust's funds for leukaemia research rose to £90,000 annually for foreign scholars alone in the 1980s.

Lady Meherbai D. Tata Education Trust (1932) also established by Sir Dorab Tata in memory of his wife, has so far disbursed Rs 11 lakh to enable women graduates to proceed abroad to study social work.

The J.R.D. Tata Trust, established in 1944, is a multipurpose trust for the advancement of learning and the relief of human suffering. It has disbursed over a crore of rupees.

The Jamsetji Tata Trust (1974) was designed to assist innovative projects and has expended considerable sums for the rehabilitation of the blind and for helping the aged. Recently it has started giving grants to J.N. Tata Scholars who receive loans from the J.N. Tata Endowment. These grants have been made possible by generous donations to the corpus of the trust by the leading Tata companies from their operating profits.

The Homi Bhabha Fellowships Council (established in 1966) is sponsored jointly by the Tata trusts and the Ford Foundation.

The last of these was launched in 1966 in memory of Dr Homi Bhabha. The programme was not for higher formal studies but for the promotion of excellence in any field of endeavour, be it research in arts, literature, social sciences, economics or technology. A handsome scholarship—and where required travelling allowance plus equipment—is also provided. Amongst its fifty recipients to date are Girish Karnad, a well-known name in the field of drama and films; Arun Shourie, the eminent journalist who is a Cabinet Minister now and the well-known journalist Prem Shankar Jha.

When the crunch of the energy crisis hit the world in 1974, Tatas, spearheaded by Tata Chemicals, founded the Tata Energy Research Institute (TERI).

In order to ensure a quick take-off, TERI identified and sponsored numerous energy research projects in various national institutions. In addition, it has set up a very large documentation centre and is supporting projects of energy scientists in the country.

The trusts have also been pioneers of rural uplift, having launched the major programme at Maan Taluka in Maharashtra in 1953 at about the same time when the government launched its Five Year Plans. Tatas' programmes of relief of distress started in 1934 with the Bihar earthquake and relief programmes have been continuous in a vast land afflicted frequently by ravages of nature plus the cruelty and indifference of man to his fellow man.

Between themselves the Tata trusts have created an infrastructure for the balanced development of the nation in science, technology and the social sciences. They have launched pace-setting institutions that have given India its first institute for social sciences, its first cancer hospital and research centre, and its first institute for fundamental research in physics and mathematics that gave India a head-on start in its atomic energy programme.

Extracted from *The Creation of Wealth: The Tatas from the 19th to the 21st Century* by R.M. Lala

Notes

Chapter 2: J.R.D. Tata

1. A partner in Tata Sons. After the family built Tata Steel, the Tata power companies and the Taj Mahal Hotel in the first decade of the twentieth century, it became India's biggest firm. But when R.D. Tata joined it in the 1870s, it was merely a medium-sized Bombay textile group.

Chapter 3: Jamsetji Tata

1. He had declined a baronetcy.
2. A 'crore' of rupees is ten million; a 'lakh' is 1,00,000.
3. In the 1980s, modernization of the Tata Steel plant of 2.1 million tonnes cost Rs 1,000 crore, and an additional capacity of 6,00,000 tonnes cost Rs 1,500 crore in the 1990s. This is not only a measure of the new technology but also indicative of the fall in the value of money.
4. There were two Ratan Tatas—one was Ratan Dadabhai Tata, the father of J.R.D. Tata, who was related to Jamsetji. The other was Jamsetji's second son, Sir Ratan. When Tata Sons was founded in 1887, the three original partners were Jamsetji, Dorab

and R.D. Tata. Jamsetji's son Ratan, quite young at the time, was made a partner later.

5. *The Economic Times*, 17 January 1979.

Chapter 4: Sir Dorabji Tata

1. Boria Majumdar and Nalin Mehta, *India and the Olympics* (New York: Routledge, 2009), p. 9.
2. 'Tata's Olympic Safari', *Times of India*, 3 August 2008, available online at: http://timesofindia.indiatimes.com/home/stoi/deep-focus/tatas-olympic-safari/articleshow/3319673.cms.
3. Boria Majumdar and Nalin Mehta, *India and the Olympics* (New York: Routledge, 2009), p. 10.
4. 'In the Name of the Father', available online at: http://www.tata.co.in/aboutus/articlesinside/!$$$!vi!$$$!KywJPS4=/TLYVr3YP-kMU=.
5. 'Dorabji Tata while Laying the Foundation Stone of the Lonavala Dam, 8 February 1911', available online at: http://www.tatasteel.com/investors/annual-report-2010-11/html/hd3.html.

Chapter 5: Sir Nowroji Saklatwala

1. 'The Man Who Played from the Heart', available online at: http://www.tata.com/aboutus/articlesinside/CPKdkBZjW3c=/TLYVr3YPkMU=.
2. Ibid.

Chapter 6: Russi Mody

1. Subrata Roy, 'Russi Mody: Businessman of the Year 1983', *Business India*, 19 December 1983–1 January 1984.
2. S.N. Pandey, *Human Side of Tata Steel* (Tata McGraw-Hill Publishing Company Ltd, 1989).
3. R.M. Lala, *Beyond The Last Blue Mountain: A Life of J.R.D. Tata* (Penguin Books India, 1993).

4. Gita Piramal, *Business Legends* (Penguin Books India, 1998).
5. Amrita Nair Ghaswalla, 'Russi Mody Was an Institution at Tata Steel: Ratan Tata', *The Hindu BusinessLine*, 17 May 2014.
6. Subrata Roy, 'Russi Mody: Businessman of the Year 1983', *Business India*, 19 December 1983–1 January 1984.
7. Meher Marfatia, 'Big House In A Little Lane', *Mid-Day*, 17 April 2016.
8. Incidentally, my ancestral family office is also located on Homi Mody Street, just 200 metres away from Bombay House.
9. In the Bihar Land Reforms Act 1956, when the Singhbhum zamindaris were taken over by the Government, an amendment was inserted exempting Jamshedpur (located in the East Singhbhum district).
10. Subrata Roy, 'Russi Mody: Businessman of the Year 1983', *Business India*, 19 December 1983–1 January 1984.
11. Palakunnathu Mathai, 'Chairman Russi Mody Completes 50 years in TISCO', *India Today*, 14 February 2013.

Chapter 7: Sumant Moolgaokar

1. In 2003, Tata Engineering and Locomotive Company (TELCO) was renamed as Tata Motors.
2. Shubha Madhukar, 'The Innovation Sanskar', *Tata Review*, April 2014.
3. Naazneen Karmali, 'Businessman of the Year 1988: Sumant Moolgaokar', *Business India*, 8 January 1989.
4. Murali Gopalan, 'The Japanese Juggernaut Rolls on beyond Maruti Too', *The Hindu BusinessLine*, 28 September 2017.
5. Telang shared several lessons that the team learnt in the making of 407. 'One was to try something new and that employees would not be punished for failure. The other was the spirit of "never say die" and to always keep fighting adversities. The teamwork was extraordinary, and the company rose to the occasion by getting ordinary people to do extraordinary tasks.'

Chapter 9: S. Ramadorai

1. Tata Consultancy Service, part of the Tata Group, is a global IT software and services company.
2. Jayant Pendharkar was one of the earliest recruits of TCS; he joined the company around the same time as Ramadorai.
3. Faqir Chand Kohli is erstwhile CEO of TCS, Ramadorai's predecessor.

Chapter 12: Taj Hotels

1. R.M. Lala, *For the Love of India: The Life and Times of Jamsetji Tata* (Penguin Books India, 2004).
2. R.M. Lala, *The Creation of Wealth: The Tatas from the 19th to the 21st Century* (Penguin Books India, 2004).
3. Ibid.
4. Other firsts by the Taj Mahal Hotel include American fans, German elevators, chandelier polishing machines, Turkish baths and English butlers. Eventually, it had Bombay's first-ever licensed bar—the Harbour Bar—India's first all-day dining restaurant, its first twenty-four-hour coffee shop and the first international discotheque.
5. As per the Tata Group website, The Indian Hotels Company Limited (IHCL) and its domestic and international subsidiaries are collectively known as the Taj Group. Hence, the chapter has been titled as the Taj Group of Hotels and includes the broad range of products and services offered by IHCL under various brands, subsidiaries and joint ventures. 'IHCL' has been primarily used to denote the company, whereas 'the Taj' has been used mostly to focus on the brand Taj Hotels Resorts and Palaces.
6. Bhakti Chughanee, 'The Grand Old Lady,' *Business India*, 6–19 January 2003.
7. The Merry Weather Road entrance of the Taj was closed for good. Finally, the front side of the hotel on Colaba Causeway

became its rear side, and the rear side near the Gateway of India became its main entrance.

8. Shyamal Majumdar, 'The Story of Taj,' *Business Standard*, 17 December 2011.

9. Charles Allen and Sharda Dwivedi, *The Taj at Apollo Bunder* (Pictor Publishing, 2010).

10. Founded in 1987 by Hafiz Muhammad Saeed, LeT is one of the largest terrorist organizations in South Asia, headquartered in Muridke near Lahore in Pakistan. It is banned by USA, the UK, the European Union and many other developed countries of the world, and sanctioned by the United Nations since 2008.

11. Built to commemorate the arrival of King George V and Queen Mary at Apollo Bunder in 1911.

12. Adrian Levy and Cathy Scott-Clark, *The Siege: 68 Hours Inside the Taj Hotel* (Penguin Books India, 2013).

13. *Condé Nast Traveller*—UK Reader's Travel Awards 2008.

14. It was established in 1932 by Sir Dorab Tata, the elder son of Jamsetji Tata. It is among the oldest philanthropic organizations in India, started with the prime purpose of encouraging learning and research and of meeting the costs of relief during crises and calamities, besides carrying out worthwhile charitable activities.

15. It was established in 1918 following the death of Sir Ratan Tata, the younger son of Jamsetji Tata. It operates in accordance with his will and gives grants to institutions in the areas of rural livelihood and communities, education, enhancing civil society and governance, health and arts and culture.

16. 'Indian Hotels forms the Taj Public Service Welfare Trust', Tata Group Media Release, 15 December 2008.

17. Since then, the trust has supported rehabilitation efforts during the 13/7 Mumbai bomb blasts, Bihar fire and cyclone, Ladakh cloud burst, Sunderbans flood, Uttarakhand cloud burst and the Jammu and Kashmir cloud burst.

18. Vinod Mahanta and Nandini Raghavendra, 'Rebuilding Scarred Lives, the Tata Way', *Economic Times*, 26 November 2009.

19. Nupur Mahajan, 'Taj ka Raj', *Business India*, 5 April 2009.

20. Raymond Bickson, 'Our Hotel was Attacked', *New York Times*, 7 February 2009.
21. Post 26/11, IHCL constituted a Crisis Management Advisory Team at the enterprise level and crisis management teams at the hotel level. All hotels are assessed by an external agency for security risks, and the crisis management teams deploy emergency preparedness/crisis management plans that are periodically tested and updated based on national and international security alerts.
22. Urvashi Seth, Kranti Vibhute and Vinod Kumar Menon, 'Mumbaikars Celebrate with Obama', *Mid-Day*, 8 November 2012.

Chapter 13: Indian Institute of Science

1. Resolution of the Government of India, Home Department, No. 434-448, Simla, 27 May 1909.
2. In 2003 there were forty-two departments.
3. He was succeeded by Dr G. Padmanaban, an eminent scientist in the department of biochemistry. The present director of the institute is Professor Goverdhan Mehta, a distinguished scientist in the Department of Organic Chemistry and former vice-chancellor of Hyderabad University.
4. In 2003 the student strength was 1700, with a faculty of 450. Two thousand research papers were produced annually.
5. The recurring grant was Rs 80 crore from the central government and another Rs 68 crore in identified research projects and about Rs 15 crore towards plan grants in 2002-2003.

Chapter 15: Tata Trusts

1. Listed in the library of the London School of Economics are publications of the Ratan Tata Foundation, and they include some early surveys on the 'Feeding of School Children' and 'Casual Labour in the Docks'. Among the researchers were

R.H. Tawney and Arthur Greenwood. These were pioneer studies of their kind.

2. This includes establishment of the Tata Memorial Centre; the Tata Institute of Social Sciences; the National Centre for the Performing Arts; the Rural Welfare Board; the Tata Institute of Fundamental Research and the National Institute for Advanced Studies.

Copyright Acknowledgements